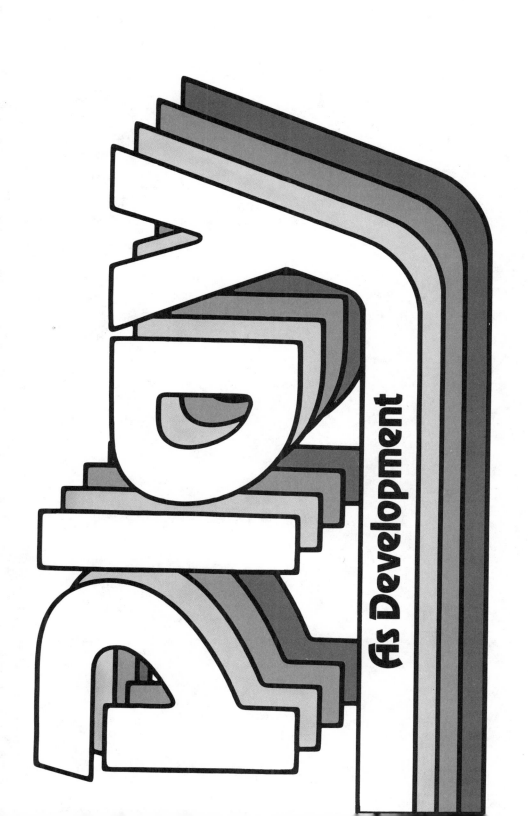

Play As Development

Annie L. Butler
Indiana University

Edward Earl Gotts
Appalachia Educational Laboratory

Nancy L. Quisenberry
Southern Illinois University

CHARLES E. MERRILL PUBLISHING COMPANY
A Bell & Howell Company
Columbus   Toronto   London   Sydney

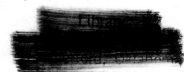

Published by
Charles E. Merrill Publishing Company
A Bell & Howell Company
Columbus, Ohio 43216

This book was set in Advertisers Gothic and Helvetica.
The production editor was Rosemary Barnett.
The cover was prepared by Will Chenoweth.
The photographs are by Celia Drake.

Library of Congress Catalog Card Number: 77–84836

International Standard Book Number: 0–675–08422–9

Printed in United States of America

2 3 4 5 6 7 8—83 82 81 80 79

Preface

During the decade of the seventies, interest in the subject of play has increased among early childhood educators. For a time during the 1960s, many early childhood educators emphasized academic learning and neglected play. Since then, interest in play has been boosted by a number of events. Such things as the work of Jean Piaget, the popularity of and interest in the British Infant School movement, and the growing interest in open education have all contributed to the rise in interest. Play is now being reconsidered and given the recognition it deserves as a learning medium for early childhood.

This book has been written in response to this rising interest in play among early childhood educators. Its aim is to fulfill this interest by offering fresh insights to the reader into the nature and functions of play and suggesting varied, illustrative, practical applications of these insights to the classroom. Part I of this book traces the history of play and describes some of the theories that regard play as a learning medium. It presents our point of view regarding what play is and how it should be guided. We consider both how play develops and how development through play can be encouraged.

Part II focuses primarily on the uses of play to promote development. In these chapters, we have not strictly followed the traditional division of learning into affective, cognitive, and psychomotor domains. Rather, we organized the discussion into, what seems to us, a more appropriate organization for the consideration of play. Since a large part of the young child's play involves some aspect of coping with the physical environment, we have devoted Chapter Three to this topic. Chapter Four takes a broad approach to the development of understanding the social environment, and Chapter Five shows the value of play for developing as an individual. In view of the recent emphasis on recreation and the wise use of leisure, we have examined, in Chapter Six, those aspects of play most relevant to creating and recreating. Several very important aspects of development to which play contributes, such as language, are not confined to any one of the preceding chapters, but can be found in all the chapters, where most appropriate to the association of language with play. We believe that development is integrated; accordingly, in each chapter, we devote some attention to the emotional and conceptual aspects of development. Since materials and toys are essential in stimulating and determining the quality of play, systematic suggestions for selecting materials are provided in Part II, Chapter Seven.

Part III deals with two special applications of play. All children, whatever their abilities or level of adjustment, have a need for the therapeutic aspects of play, although some have a greater need for it than others. The therapeutic aspect of play is not necessarily limited to situations involving psychologists or psychiatrists, so it is important for educators to be aware of these aspects. The last chapter discusses how play can be used to provide maximum value in the educational program for kindergarten and primary children. Moreover, this chapter suggests a new and workable approach to unifying the school learning environment from kindergarten through third grade.

Throughout the book, we have tried to show in an understandably written form how play develops, its potential values, and how it can be stimulated and guided. We feel that such an approach should be helpful to teachers in nursery schools, child care centers, kindergartens, and primary grades. Prospective teachers now enrolled in two-year and four-year instructional programs, teachers in inservice programs, special education teachers wishing to use play in the preschool and primary years, and parents who want to understand and guide their own children's play will find this approach useful. Parents will find considerable material on infancy as well as the preschool and primary years.

In several chapters we alternated the use of the generic "he" or "she" to refer to the singular "child." This provides some desirable variety from the practice of always writing in plural or arranging sentences to avoid the use of "he" and, thus, promotes a more readable book. We believe that this will be understood by our readers as a reasonable literary device—not to be confused with sex stereotyping which, we believe, is notably absent from our thinking and writing.

One of the challenges of writing this book has been the opportunity to bring together our mutual interest and background in child development and early childhood education with our interest in play as a means of facilitating development and learning. This is the third writing project on which we have worked jointly in an attempt to encourage educational programs consistent with the developmental abilities of children. We hope that these efforts will facilitate a better fit between children's abilities and the educational programs provided for them.

Contents

PLAY AND ITS ROLE IN DEVELOPMENT

I

The following two chapters of Part I examine several important questions about play.

- What is its nature and what are its functions? Does all play emerge spontaneously? How much of it is learned?
- What helpful insights do scholars have into why children play and how have the major theories sought to explain it?
- What do we know about the history of play? For example, has play changed over the centuries? Is it changing now?
- Why is play emphasized in early childhood education and should this emphasis be changed?
- Does children's play vary in relation to their levels of development? If so, what is play like at each level?
- Does play affect development and, if so, in what areas?
- Does play influence development differently as the child matures? Do play needs change with age?

And subsequently—

- How great is the importance, and what specifically is the place of play in early childhood development and education?

Part I explores these questions and provides the background and foundation required for an informed, insightful application of play theory to early childhood practice and to parenting.

CHAPTER
ONE

*Handling, grasping, and exploring develops
with action patterns.*

Play Reconsidered – to Play Is to Develop

Psychologists, teachers and educators have questioned and studied the role of play in child development in many ways. Through the ages societies have accepted play as a childhood activity and in some cases as an activity only for the more privileged classes. There has been no agreement, however, on how long play should be a function of the child's life or how important it is to development.

In some societies children were pushed to carry out adult tasks at a very early age. Some had to forsake play as we know it today for work in the mines, the mills, the fields, or the home. Because it took all available family members to earn enough money for food, clothing, and shelter, children had to work. Life necessitated such an existence.

Later, when making a living required fewer persons and less effort, there was more leisure time for both children and adults. Thus, children had more time to play, and adults had more time to pursue their own leisure activities.

This chapter looks at how history has viewed play, at the importance educators and developmental psychologists place on play, and at our view of play as it relates to both home and school.

Play Defined

The definition of play changes with the perception of the individual defining it. Because children bring a set of experiences, thoughts, and feelings about themselves and others to the play situation, and because play does not exist in isolation, a formal definition is difficult. Also, depending upon the individual viewpoint, play may be seen either as something useful to learning and to developmental processes or as something trivial and non-essential. In this book, we define *play* by behaviors that are prevalent or abounding at particular ages. Beyond this, it is defined as a design for development. That is, that in addition to defining play by what a child does, it can be shown how different play activities help a child develop cognitively, physically, and socially.

Too often our society's view of play restricts it to exercises and games or only those activities involving motor development. But play also includes those activities that contribute to the social growth of the person and to his ability to recreate the society in which he lives. This conception of play has led to its being defined in various ways by psychologists and educators. Social psychologists study play in terms of the need children have to prepare for their later role in adult society. Educators advocate the role of play in facilitating learning. These points of view must be assessed, however, in the context of the historical era in which they exist, for society determines the acts of play as well as the view of play.

A Historical Perspective. Play is often considered one of the most important aspects of childhood. Let us look at this idea from an historical perspective. By the Renaissance, childhood, in the context of a developmental stage as we know it today, had essentially been lost. The small child was treated as a miniature adult. We can see this in paintings of young boys in replicas of men's clothing and young girls in dresses that were replicas of women's dresses. Children were expected to step into adult roles as soon as they were physically able. Boys took up the sword and shield as soon as they could hold them, girls ground meal or spun cloth; and the children of serfs worked alongside their parents in the fields.

Stone presents an interesting discussion of the development of play through the centuries in "The Play of Little Children." [24] He indicates that childhood did not exist prior to the seventeenth century. That is, children were expected to act as little adults and taught to carry out adult tasks. The life of Louis XIII is an example. According to Stone, Louis was singing and playing the violin by seventeen months. He was dancing various dances by two, and he could read by three and write by four. And Louis XIII was not considered particularly brilliant. Paintings of that time reveal the identical clothing styles of children and adults. There was play. Louis XIII did have toys, as did people in all levels of society. One can see in reports of leisure activities of this period that adults and children took part in festivals and games. But the purposes of such play, as Stone points out, were different for children than for adults. Children were learning their roles for society in their play. Adults used attendance at festivals and gaming events for relaxation and a break from their work.

Play gradually came to have more of a role in the life of children in seventeenth and eighteenth century European society. In English society, however, play behaviors were generally suppressed. By the end of the 18th Century, in England, play spaces were unavailable and playing in the streets was prohibited.

Play in America during the seventeenth and eighteenth centuries varied with the geographic location and the ethnic orgin of the population. Play was disguised in work-related activities, such as barn-raisings and quilting parties. Since early American religions stressed the necessity of work, and the Puritan influences stressed the avoidance of pleasure associated with play, both England and America released children from work much later than France.

As people of western societies began to recognize the existence of play they attempted to define and explain it. Before the nineteenth century, a major theoretical position was the "surplus energy" theory. It was thought that children, like young animals, have a surplus of energy which has to be used up. Groos believed that beginning with the primitive features of behavior, those features that relive the past development of humanity, the child passes through various stages in which biologically important impulses are worked through in order for the child to move on to adult life. The child must work through all impulses which are biologically important, but which are now useless and inconsistent with conditions of modern life.

Around the turn of the century, Groos proposed another theory on children's play.[11] Based on his observations of animals and on his observation of his own children, Groos concluded that the activities in which children engaged provided them with practice for acquiring physical and social skills for use in later life. But McLellan suggests that this theory is questionable because play often seems to be an activity undertaken for its own sake, and so far as adults can perceive, is not always directed to a particular end.[16] Thus, while some play activity may lead to adult skills, much of it is appropriate only for a short period of the child's life.

Hall proposed yet another theory on play. Based on his developmental psychology background and Darwin's theory, which was very popular at the time, Hall's ideas showed the child as playing out each successive stage of the human race.[12] Other authors have raised some questions regarding his theory, in reference to animals—young animals usually must look for their own food within a relatively short time after birth. Yet, they still play while maintaining their food supply. Also children must take time to rest and have difficulty staying with the same task for a long time, which raises some doubts about whether or not children actually have an energy surplus.[16] Children play for many reasons. To be rid of excess energy is only one possible explanation since play meets many other needs as well. Hall insisted that children learn best through spontaneous play. He turned to Froebel for support for his theory.

Froebel described play as the highest expression of human development in childhood.[10] Play, he believed, was the one free expression of what is in a child's soul, and to Froebel, play was the purest and most spiritual product of the child. He recognized it as a type of and copy of human life at all stages and in all relations, teaching that one who has insight into human nature can see the child reveal the trends of his future life in the way in which he plays. Froebel understood the role of play in the development of the child, although he never actually worked out a classification system on play as play.

Piaget provides us with a cognitive theory of play. In *Play, Dreams and Imitation In Childhood,* he relates play in its initial stages to assimilation.[21] In Piaget's theory, play derives from the child working out two fundamental characteristics of his mode of experience and development. This refers to *accommodation* and *assimilation.* According to his theory, the child integrates new experiences or environmental information into his existing cognitive structure through *assimilation. Accommodation* is the creation of new structures made necessary by newly assimilated information. Piaget classified these two distinctive behavioral tendencies, representative of two poles of intellectual thought, as *play* and *imitation.* He defined *play* as a continuation of assimilation and *imitation* as a continuation of accommodation.

Piaget describes play, in its initial stages, as the pole of the behaviors defined by assimilation. Almost all of the behaviors studied in relationship to intelligence are susceptible to becoming play as soon as they are repeated for mere assimilation, that is, when they occur for functional pleasure.[21]

Practice play, according to Piaget, begins in the first months of a child's life. Symbolic play occurs during the second year, however, games with rules rarely occur before the second stage (ages 4-7) and belong primarily to the third stage (ages 7-11). These play stages parallel Piaget's description of the development of intelligence. He says that the explanation for the late appearance and protracted continuation of games with rules is really very simple. He considers them the *ludic,* or play-related, activity of a socialized being. In other words, just as the symbol replaces mere practice as soon as thought appears, so the rule replaces the symbol and integrates practice as soon as certain social relationships are formed. More will be said about age differences in play in the next chapter.

If we follow Piaget's theory, we can see that the evolution of children's play follows three successive stages: practice, symbolism, and rules. These stages have various relationships to constructional or creative games that must also be considered. The disappearance of practice games occurs when play is reintegrated into adaptive activity. In other cases, mere practice may become symbolic or become coupled with symbolism. This change can occur when a sensorimotor schema changes into a symbolic schema, or when the constructions that emerge from play-related combinations lead to symbolic imitation instead of becoming adaptive activity or work. In the latter instance, practice games may acquire rules by becoming collective, and thus evolve into a game with rules.

Piaget views games from the perspective of the three successive stages that he relates to the three stages of intelligence (sensorimotor, representational, and reflective). However, he considers constructional games separate from the three stages because they occupy the second, and more particularly, the third level. He describes this as a position halfway between play and intelligent work, or between play and imitation.

Sutton-Smith approaches the definition of play from a different perspective. He thinks that disservice to play is more likely if the descriptive concepts are derived from ego-functions, cognitions, etc., than if they are drawn from games. Drawing from studies by Redl, Gump, and Roberts, he describes a formal game in the form of an exercise of voluntary control systems.[23] In this activity, there is a contest between powers (individuals or teams). The activity is confined by rules in an order which produces a disequilibrial outcome. That is, someone wins and someone loses.[23] The term, *confinement by rules*, refers to the fact that games prescribe the roles, the interaction patterns, the performances, and the procedures for action as well as the time- and space-related contexts.

Let us look at Sutton-Smith's discussion of play in terms of game elements. First, the element of *purpose* stresses that we are discussing play-related purposes, not the player's psychological or sociologically derived motives. Both are relevant to a total understanding of play but not to an understanding of the structure of play. He proposes that if games are a contest of powers, then it would follow that play is a *test* of powers. That is, it is a test of cognitive, affective, and conative powers. This means that children test their abilities. This view fits with the oft-repeated idea that the pleasure in play is the pleasure of function, or the pleasure of mastery of a task or an activity. A first step in an analysis of play might therefore be a cataloging of the powers to be tested. These tested powers are largely motor and sensory in infancy with symbolic elements of play increasing in early childhood. In later childhood and adulthood, the focus is on testing physical and strategic powers.[23]

The second element Sutton-Smith analyzes is the *actor-counteractor relationship*. He applies this idea to infants' reversals of action. That is, the infant reverses his own behavior to interact with his environment differently. Although Piaget recognized the repetition in this "play" behavior, Sutton-Smith observed the change from earlier actions. What appears to be imitative action by the two year old could be adaptive behavior to some incongruous counterpart. By the time the child is three, the reversals are indeed a part of play. The child uses other voices in solitary play which interact in conversations he projects. By the fourth year miniature social systems emerge as well as imaginary characters. From ages four to seven, the action and counteraction is social in nature with play taking the form of people in houses, trucks, shops, etc. Even in the *central-person* games of childhood (race, chase, attack, hide, capture, search, rescue) one sees the reciprocal relationships between actors and counteractors.[23]

Although these parts of Sutton-Smith's theory are not so fully developed, he explains that the elements of performance and spatiotemporal (space and time) controls are important considerations in play as well as in games. Types of performance—motor, language, intellectual, emotive, body contact, and body movement—are required game elements.[23]

The *outcome of play* is also an important consideration. In terms of Piaget's theory, the outcome of games is unbalanced, that is, someone wins and someone else loses. Sutton-Smith argues that the intention of play is to do something differently. This difference might be to make a unique response to a customary circumstance or to cause events to move away from their cognitive or affective equilibrium. Further study and observation is needed on the unique transformations that occur in play before the theory of play as a disequilibrium phenomenon can be fully understood.

The "play way" schools in the United States and in Great Britain are often attributed to the progressive ideas of Dewey. No discussion of play definitions would be complete without an examination of his ideas. American schools of the 1920's and 1930's were greatly influenced by Dewey. During World War II and postwar years in England, his ideas were credited for changes in their school system, particularly at the "infant school (primary school) level."

Dewey maintained that imitation is only one means by which the child learns. Adults in the child's environment supply rich, varied, complex, and even novel stimuli to which the child reacts. The child selects from the stimuli, finds what can be successfully used, and continues to use that which has value or discards that which has no value. The child acquires skills not merely by imitation but by a combination of attention, observation, selection, experimentation, and confirmation of results.[5]

Play is more than mere physical activity. Dewey points out that as the child plays he builds up a storehouse of concepts and a world of meanings, all of which are essential to intellectual growth.

As children play house, store, school, or doctor, they organize and arrange meanings and concepts into groups of familiar information. Thus, these meanings are made to cohere in connected ways. Even the "freest" of play observes some principles of unification and coherence.[5] As Plato and Froebel declared earlier, play is the mode of education for the child in later years of infancy.

Dewey differentiates between *playfulness* and *play*. The former, he says, is an attitude of mind. In order to avoid having play terminate only in arbitrary fantasy and building up an imaginary world alongside the world of actuality, the play attitude must gradually pass into a work attitude. It is here we find the idea of separating play from work, and here also that we distinguish attitudes of play and work from performance.

Work, as Dewey uses it, denotes more than its usual definition. It is more than mere routine activity or simply doing things that need to be done. It originates from the inside, as thought-guided activity when the person sets out to accomplish something. In this sense, it signifies ingenuity and inventiveness by selecting the right means for accomplishing the task. It includes making plans and testing them on the basis of actual results.

This highly intelligent action manifested in the child is highly educative. This is not the result of the repetition of teacher-prescribed work or drills, either oral or written. It is educative because it allows the child to test meaning and continually build meaning in actual situations. Dewey maintains that the true distinction between work and play is not an interest in activity for its own sake or interest in an external result of that activity, but it is in fact between an interest as it flows from moment to moment, and an interest in an activity tending to culmination. This latter involves tending to the thread of continuity that binds the activity together as it passes from stage to stage to the outcome. Unfortunately, too many educators failed to understand Dewey's theory and used the play concept instead of the work concept he advocated.

Value of Play

The value of play to the life of a child can be measured in cognitive, affective, and psychomotor terms. Perhaps the most obvious and most quickly accepted is its value to physical development. It is easy to see physical skills develop in a child as a result of practicing running, hopping, weaving, or threading beads. It is not always easy to see such development in the cognitive and affective aspects of a child's life. The following paragraphs briefly discuss possible relationships between play and development in cognitive and affective areas, thereby providing an overview. Part II of this book attempts to make these connections more systematically.

In learning about adult roles children are discovering the meaning of the adult world. In their play, they practice the real tasks and roles they will later assume. Although play often provides a clash of wills, this experience is of great value in learning to cope with others.

Early psychoanalytic theories accepted a cathartic principle in play that allowed the child to work off pent-up emotions and find relief for past frustrations. A child who feels unable to regulate the activities in his life may find relief in play. For instance, the child whose parent must leave to go to work may transfer pent-up frustrations to an object which can be made to come and go at will. In contrast to the adult who can talk out his frustrations, the child must act or "play" his feelings out.

All children go through periods of throwing things, hitting, kicking at blocks and other toys, screaming and actually destroying things. But this behavior usually does not continue long. Generally, children turn to more creative and constructive behavior with people and with toys.

Inherent in the play of the child is the potential for mental exercise which the child creates for himself. Piaget's work is probably most often cited as influencing the belief that children come to learn, understand, and achieve intellectual success through interaction with their environment. As Arnaud points out, by virtue of its spontaneous, highly pleasurable qualities, play acts as an energizer and organizer of cognitive learning.[2]

As thoughts and cognitive processes form and take structure, children test their knowledge in play situations. This testing process provides refinement of and development in a full range of skills, including language, motor, perception, memory, concept formation, reality testing, and secondary-process thinking.[18]

Many educators believe that both children and animals who are deprived of play do not learn as effectively as those children and animals who have the freedom to explore and to manipulate materials in their environment. They are also concerned that the recently designed, structured, cognitively oriented programs may not be sufficient for true cognitive growth, particularly for the younger child. These programs do not allow the child to explore or make decisions about the use of materials or equipment. They establish rote learning very early. Both Piaget and Dewey show the need for young children to interact with their environment in order to internalize and integrate their experiences into their own cognitive structures.

Play seems to be a motivating factor in children's intellectual learning. This motivation can be observed in their repetitious behaviors and and from continued success in their endeavors which generates other spontaneous behavior. Because of the spontaneous aspect of play and the enjoyment which children find in it, learning is a natural outcome of many of these endeavors.

The effect of experience and environment upon child development has been repeatedly recognized by educators, psychologists, biologists and others concerned with child growth and development. Erikson, a psychologist and practicing psychoanalyst, developed an outline of the eight stages of development which contribute to a healthy personality. The eight stages identified by Erikson lead to a sense of trust, autonomy, initiative, accomplishment, identity, intimacy, parenting, and integrity.[7] Three of these stages are important to consider in this study of play. They are autonomy, initiative, and the sense of accomplishment.

According to Erikson, at about the age of twelve to fifteen months, after the sense of trust is established, the struggle for a sense of autonomy begins.[7] For the next two years, the child works to assert that he is a human being with a mind and a will of his own. The child is struggling to be independent, yet at the same time needs the help and guidance of adults. The outcome of this struggle, hopefully, will be self-control without loss of self-esteem. Undesirable outcomes would be doubt and shame.

Since this is the period for muscle-system maturation, the ability to coordinate a number of highly conflicting action patterns—holding on and letting go, walking, talking, and manipulating objects—develops in the child at the same time. A pressing need to use these abilities—to handle, to grasp, to drop, to explore—develops concurrently with action-pattern development. There is a persistent urge to do it alone, and consequently, there is the need to handle the frustration that comes with the inability to use hands and feet effectively.

In order to develop the sense of autonomy, the child must have the opportunity to make choices and to practice over and over again to learn what can or cannot be done. Parental regulations and assistance is necessary for some essential behaviors, but firm, consistent parents who allow exploration and self-determination add to the child's feeling of self-worth.

After achieving a feeling of individuality and enjoying this feeling for a year or so, the four- or five-year-old child begins seeking an identity. In trying to understand parents and other adults, the child imitates their actions and occupations. We see this behavior when a child imitates the postman, the bus driver, a parent or a television character. During this period, much learning takes place that leads away from the child's own limitations and opens up a wealth of future possibilities. Extended interaction with other children and with adults takes place, as well as vigorous physical activity.

Parents and teachers need to be aware of the development of conscience during this stage. Children begin to feel guilt for both real and imagined thoughts and actions. At this stage, they attempt to learn how to will without feeling guilt. They dream up many things that adults tell them not to do or that they cannot do. They find that many of their ideas are impossible to execute, and that others do not win the approval of the adults around them.[7]

It is very important that children have the opportunity to play and to develop this initiative. Too much restriction may result in a bitter, vindictive attitude and an unhealthy personality. Erikson says that a child, who has the opportunity to get some sense of the roles and function one can perform as an adult, can progress happily to the next stage of development. Thus, we see that the development of initiative is closely tied to the development of play in the child.

The next stage, the sense of accomplishment, is important for primary teachers to understand. It begins at about age six and extends through the next five years. It sometimes is referred to as the *stage of industry.*[7] This is the period when the imagination seems to settle down and the child wants to learn how to do things and how to do them well.

This is an important period in the child's life because it lays a sound foundation for good citizenship and for acquiring knowledge and skills which lead to good workmanship. He learns to cooperate with others and to follow rules. Because children need to feel a sense of accomplishment during this period, schools need to provide programs that meet individual needs. In this respect, they must guard against the child's developing feelings of failure or inadequacy.

During the 1960s, a number of early childhood, compensatory programs were developed that had a high cognitive orientation. These highly directed programs, which allowed little or no time for play, were developed and put into practice throughout the country. Advocates of these programs were challenged in articles encouraging free play or activity times in classrooms. The debate over the role of play in kindergarten now raged through the nursery schools. By the mid-1970s, an increasing awareness of the role of play in the child's cognitive development once again prevailed. But one cannot ignore the fact that in the United States our background has dictated that play and learning are not synonymous. But neither are work and play opposite ends of a continuum. Children's activity may be judged differently from one time to another depending upon the age and/or purposes of the child. The distinctions between the philosophies, however, often appear in nursery school, kindergarten, and primary school. Much work still needs to be done to make educators realize that play is essential to learning and is indeed a vehicle for learning.

Our view of play is drawn from the theories discussed previously. We believe that play is an important means by which the child develops, and that development is the result of play activity throughout childhood. In essence, what children typically and spontaneously do is what promotes their development. This view of play will be further developed in Chapter Two.

How Play Is Used

While the practitioners questioned the role of play, theorists consistently stressed its value. Freud indicated that not only is play the means by which the child accomplishes his first great cultural and psychological achievements, but it is also his language of expression and communication.[9] Children learn through play that feelings can be safely expressed and that aggression and hostility can be controlled and managed. They learn that this kind of energy can be used constructively.[3]

Psychotherapists have long advocated the use of *play therapy*—therapy which allows the child to work out frustrations and anxiety through play—to reduce anxiety in children and to help them through normal developmental conflicts. In the child's personal life, interactions with other children lessens egocentrism and helps in developing empathy for others.

We value play for enhancing physical development in the child. Both fine and gross motor skills develop through activities and games. Coordination and following rules, from the early ages through grade school, are fostered through play.

Piaget's work has influenced early childhood educators to accept the value of play in cognitive development.[23] His studies show that through play children come to understand and master their environment. The level of mastery is, of course, related to their age and state of development, but over time their interactions with their environment bring them to a higher level of intellectual understanding.

This notion is reinforced by Pavenstedt and Smilansky's work with disadvantaged children. Their work shows that children from deprived environments need to and can be taught how to play.

In *The Drifters,* Pavenstadt describes how a group of preschoolers changed during a two year nursery school experience. Initially, they did not know how to play.[20] But over a period of time they did begin to play and developed the capacity to enjoy it and become involved. More about this work will be covered in Chapter Four.

Smilansky's work with Israeli children indicates that disadvantaged children are poorly equipped with verbal, cognitive, and social abilities relevant to play and lack training and encouragement in the basic techniques of sociodramatic play.[22] She believes that the kindergarten can and should provide disadvantaged children with techniques for playing, and that sociodramatic play, which we will talk about in Chapter Four, can be used to develop abilities that are essential for the culturally deprived child.

Adults, too, need to know how to play. Adult play is much more ritualized and rule oriented and is generally considered leisure-time activity. Many adults, however, do not know how to play possibly as a result of a life dominated by work ethics during their formative years. With the imminent development of the four-day work week and a higher standard of living, many adults will find a need to sit back, relax, and play.

A critical factor in adult play is a balance between pleasure and displeasure. All of us will experience some displeasure in our lives at some time. We must be able to to maintain a balance of pleasurable activities to off-set the unpleasant activities. Lorenz has expressed concern for a disequilibration of the mechanism which insures this balance.[15] He cites three symptoms which give evidence of this condition in our society. The first is the urge for instant gratification. Many adults, young and old, do not have long-range goals nor are they willing to set long-range goals. A second symptom is a general inability to endure any kind of pain or displeasure. The extended often uncontrolled use of drugs, both legal and illegal, in our society and others is indicative of this symptom. The third symptom which Lorenz cites is a general unwillingness to move. By this, he means avoiding the use of muscles, opportunities to exercise, and physical labor. Our technological advances have contributed to the use of elevators and escalators and automatic car windows and garage door openers instead of using our own power to maneuver the stairs or the garage door.

The result of this disequilibration, according to Lorenz, is boredom. Part of the problem lies in the dysfunction of the mechanism which ordinarily transmits cultural norms of social behavior from one generation to the next, that is, the means by which one generation transmits a life style to the next generation. The rapid change of life-styles, occupations, and use of leisure time has necessitated change in the processes of cultural transmission. Many families spend little time together and adult leisure time is spent away from the children, e.g., they, adults, have parties as opposed to family outings. As recently as twenty or thirty years ago, family leisure time was spent together in family-oriented activities. Now, in many instances, parents engage in expensive hobbies and interests and leave their children to fend for themselves with mechanized toys. What worked for the older generation is often inappropriate for the next generation.[15]

Erikson discusses the differences between childhood play offerings and the traditional ritualizations adolescents offer to one another.[8] These ritualizations are based on both learned and perceived roles manifested by young people. He wonders if these adolescents will have learned to be playful, and therefore, able to better anticipate some leeway of personal and social development. He indicates, that in the developmental sequence, children move from childhood play through juvenile role experimentation into a dominant means of production. According to Erikson, the adult invests his playfulness and his search for identity in a daily necessity to work for the good of his human group.

Erikson shows us through discussion of adult behaviors that in order to be truly adult, one must renew, on each level, some of the playfulness of childhood and some of the sportiveness of the juvenile. Both children and adolescents show by their actions that they want to deal with concerns of central importance for settling their past and anticipating their future. The adults must always maintain a playfulness which grows with and through the adult stages of life. The ideal would be the combination of one's avocation with a vocation.

Two basic points of view exist toward the concept of leisure. One of these is the theory derived from the Greek aristocrats, who were freed from work by the use of slaves. They advocated the use of nonwork time to develop the mind, the conscience, and the good life. This idea is developed by deGrazia in his volume, *On Time, Work and Leisure,* in which he describes leisure as an end, as contemplation, joy, scholarship, or something beyond the material base or value.[4] This is the notion of *paidai,* which means all of these things put together into a life-style or personal pursuit. The second point of view considers leisure as therapy, rest, relaxation, and social control, re-creation for subsequent productive effort which is generally instrumental in character. This view is grounded in the work ethic and post-Helenic Christianity, and in the last century has broadened into a symbol for the rich.[14]

These two viewpoints have blended to become a current holistic tendency to look at leisure as an end in itself and as a means of relaxation and revitalization. The Russians, in particular, support this point of view, speaking openly of leisure time as potential for personality growth rather than as time for potential service to the socialist society.[14]

In this discussion of leisure, we can see a return to the question of what play means in the life of a child. Some see it as an end in itself; others see it as supporting the development of the child. Although leisure takes many forms other than play, the purposes are parallel. Just as play is important in the life of the child, leisure is important in the life of the adult.

Orthner stresses the need for all people to have some free time from their normal duties and responsibilities in order to actualize their inner needs, to relax, and to develop personally.[19] In recent years, changes in lifestyles due to women's liberation movements, a reduction in working hours, higher education, and many other factors have contributed to a more companionate family style. The use of leisure has become of primary importance to the adjustment of many modern families. Time spent together in leisure type activities often builds a cohesive family unit.

Thus, it appears that the need to play is necessary at all stages of life.

Although it may take different forms to meet different needs, play is a vital activity for the growing, maturing person. It affects the social, cognitive, and physical growth of the individual.

Why Children Play

Children play in an effort to understand and master their environment. Play provides an avenue through which they can have repeated experiences which help them to master cognitive, physical, and social skills. Almy cites evidence that both children and animals who are deprived of opportunities for play do not learn as effectively as those who have had the freedom to manipulate and explore.[1] The child who knows how to play is better able to advance to new stages of mastery in relating to his peers and in playing with his toys and equipment. Real progress is not just mastery of a toy or piece of equipment, but rather the understanding of where it all fits into the physical and social environment.

Unless children suffer from some abnormality or are placed in a restricted environment, they cannot seem to help playing. When materials and toys are left for their exploration, their curiosity and inquisitive attitudes lead them to examine and manipulate. The same is true for their contacts with peer-age children and adults. They will ask questions and discuss the environment even when the adult does not want to be bothered, or a peer age child does not want to play. The interaction of the child with the environment can be quite intense.

Play permits children to display their feelings. These may be feelings that reflect anxiety, hostility, or aggression, or feelings that reflect happiness and satisfaction. Young children display many kinds of behaviors and feelings. Play allows them to learn to handle the variety of feelings one has to cope with throughout life. Children learn to cope with emotions which might otherwise cause serious problems later on. They learn ways to "safely" express their feelings and to control and manage feelings of hostility and aggression.

Children also play in order to express themselves creatively. Role playing allows for creativity as well as for displaying feelings. Building structures with blocks and Tinker Toys, as well as singing, dancing, and working with art, provide children with creative, expressive outlets. Rough materials such as wood, seeds, and rocks are often used to create a toy or prop for children's play. Creative play of this nature allows children to determine how much control they have over this element of their environment. This includes both cognitive and physical control. Through manipulation of ideas and mental images, they gain control of the cognitive aspects of control; through manipulation of the materials, they gain certain fine motor skills.

In conclusion, children play to master many skills. The development of coordination of both fine and gross motor skills is a normal activity for children.

What appears to be play, even in an infant, is often serious effort to gain control of motor activities. In fact, it is often difficult to tell from observation whether a child is practicing a skill or repeating an activity purely for pleasure.

Spontaneous and Directed Play

Spontaneous play is a universal phenomenon among young children. Inherent in this play are the subtle ways in which children assign and assume roles, communicate nonverbally, and develop rules.[18] Ideas and imagination come from the child's own interests. Children seem to be endowed with the ability to use whatever is at hand to represent the features and functions of the props they need for their play.

The question of the value of spontaneous play came under consideration again after the development of the heavily prescribed cognitive programs of the 1960s. Since most of the traditional nursery schools prior to the 1960s based their programs on psychoanalytic theories of play, the emotional aspects of play were more pervasive than the intellectual aspects. The play materials and equipment in these schools allowed for maximum social inter- action among the children. The materials also provided opportunities for large muscle activity and for freedom of movement, thus relieving a build-up of tension in the children's bodies. Nursery educators considered the needs of the child to release emotional conflicts through play and provided ample opportunity for spontaneous play in the classroom.

A recognition of the need for intellectual development through play does not necessitate directed play, however. Piaget, Erikson, Sutton-Smith, and Dewey lead us to question the value of learning that takes place in a highly directed situation. Since children relate the reality of their surroundings to their egocentric and affective ways in order to arrive at the level of logical thinking found in adults, they must have the opportunity to develop through repeated, self-directed experiences. It could be argued that not only does spontaneous play provide children with the opportunity for practice and assimilation, but it also allows them to confront their environment and to accomodate to it.

What, then, is spontaneous play and how is it used by children? *Sponta- neous play* is that action or activity which children initiate on their own. This may be jumping across cracks in the sidewalk, hopping around the room, or pushing or pulling a toy. It may be building with blocks or Tinker Toys. It could be organizing other children into a game with impromptu rules. The spontaneity comes from within the child or group of children.

The opposite of spontaneous play is *directed play*. The direction may come from the toy itself. For example, a puzzle may only be put together or taken apart. The way a puzzle is used is predetermined. In some cases, the direction comes from the child, such as the child who uses a toy in only one way and will not deviate, although the same toy may be used in other ways by other children.

Montessori believed that the child learns as a result of interacting with the environment. Her method of teaching young children is a good example of a highly prepared environment. It provides for self-selected and self-directed activities within that prepared environment.[17] A Montessori classroom contains extensive apparatus and self-teaching materials. Children are encouraged to select their own activities. The "directress" (teacher) observes and is at hand to help if needed.

One can see that given the definitions of spontaneous and directed, all sorts of combinations are possible. (Also, it should be stated that this idea of spontaneous play versus directed play does not indicate opposite ends of a continuum. Depending upon the circumstances, an example of either may vary in definition. For example, a child may spontaneously choose to work a puzzle, or a teacher may draw a creative dramatics group into the housekeeping corner, and then let what actually happens be spontaneous.) The important thing is that adults realize when structure is being set and how rigidly it is being adhered to. Playing must be a creative experience that provides a basic form for living. Only when children are free to use their whole personalities, can they discover their identities.

The Adult Role in Play

The adult role in children's play activity is a critical factor. Adults can enhance or hinder children in their play. Too often, in the highly directed situation, the adult decides the time and place and provides the materials used, thus eliminating any opportunity for decision making on the child's part. Adults should strive to provide a balance between direction and spontaneity, thus allowing the child's inquisitiveness and imagination to flourish.

Learning is more intense when appropriate stimulation is given at the appropriate time. Thus, parents and other adults can intervene and provide play stimulation that will enhance and foster the child's development. The adult is the conveyor of cultural values. The interpretation, labels, and general information which adults supply are invaluable to the child, especially when play is in progress, and the child meets a problem that is too difficult to solve alone. Often a question or a suggestion from a parent or teacher is just the stimulus needed to carry on with the play.

This is different from the adult who takes over and organizes the child's play so that the child has no options. There is no chance for the child to try things out independently, to choose materials and toys to play with, and no opportunity to learn from mistakes.

Adults do need to protect children from unreasonable bullying and teasing by other children. They can also be protected by advocating safety procedures and warning them not to attempt to climb to unsafe heights or use tools and equipment in unsafe ways.

Verbal interaction with adults is vital for children. They need the stimulation of adult language and ideas and adults need to listen to children and share ideas with them. Children need to hear their ideas expressed in adult sentences. Listening to stories also helps the child.

Adults must be alert to their own behaviors that could decrease or destroy spontaneity and creativity in children. The manner in which you interact with children should be considered. One factor which must always be taken into consideration is the child's own temperament and personality. An act of encouragement to one child might be detrimental to another. A meek, timid child cannot be handled like a boisterous, aggressive child is handled. Some children need to be encouraged to use art materials at the art table, although others spend all of their time there and need to be encouraged to try other activities. The wise teacher will guide and direct only as much as needed and try to interest a child in different activities from time to time.

In order to preserve spontaneity in a child or in a classroom, rigid patterns or plans must be avoided. Carefully prescribed activities should be questioned. For example, avoid art activities for which an example of the finished product is shown to the children; physical activities in which each child stands in line to take his turn and walk or run in a prescribed way; math materials which have written drills with no opportunity for experimentation and manipulation; and creative dramatics activities in which the action is directed. The list is endless. Avoidance of specific models when creativity is desired is always a good rule to follow.

Although specific help and direction may need to be given from time to time to a child with a special problem, much can be done to keep creativity and imagination flowing. A wide variety of materials with adequate freedom of choice aids greatly in preserving spontaneity in the classroom.

Limits of Play

Play does not mean the same thing to everybody. Dewey considered play to be a means by which children develop physically, cognitively, and emotionally, but because he knew that some people saw play as useless and time-consuming, he felt the need to describe some aspects of play as "work" in order to have his ideas accepted by kindergarten and primary teachers. An environment void of materials, equipment, and peers certainly would not enhance a child's growth toward adulthood in our culture. For play to have value, it must be supported by materials, and by guidance from parents and teachers or caregivers, and adequate basic experiences. Interaction with others is as important as interaction with objects in the environment. Without this, verbal communication skills are retarded.

Finally, problem solving processes can be developed. Play activities provide the opportunity for children to try out what they have learned so that problem solving can take place spontaneously. At the same time, strategies for solving problems can be worked through with the children. These learning experiences can actually enhance the spontaneous ones.

NOTES

1. Millie Almy, *Early Childhood Play: Selected Readings Related to Cognition and Motivation* (New York: Simon and Schuster, 1968).

2. Sara H. Arnaud, "Some Functions of Play In the Educative Process," *Childhood Education* 51, (November/December, 1974): 72-78.

3. Joan Cass, *The Significance of Children's Play* (London: B. T. Batsford, 1971).

4. Sebastian De Grazia, *Of Time Work and Leisure* (New York: Twentieth Century Fund, 1962).

5. John Dewey, *How We Think,* (Chicago: Henry Regnery Company, 1933).

6. Erik H. Erikson, *Childhood and Society* (New York: W. W. Norton and Company, Inc., 1963).

7. Erik H. Erikson, "A Healthy Personality for Every Child," in Millie Almy, *Early Childhood Play: Selected Readings Related To Cognition and Motivation* (New York: Simon and Schuster, 1968).

8. Erik H. Erikson, "Play and Actuality," in Maria W. Piers, Ed., *Play and Development* (New York: W. W. Norton and Company, Inc., 1972).

9. Sigmund Freud, *Beyond The Pleasure Principle,* Standard edition, 18 (London: Hogarth, 1955).

10. Friedrich Froebel, *Chief Writings on Education,* trans. S. S. Fletcher and J. Welton (London: Arnold, 1912).

11. Karl Groos, *The Play of Man* (New York: Appleton, 1901).

12. G. Stanley Hall, *Aspects of Childlife and Education* (London and Boston: Ginn and Company, 1907).

13. G. Stanley Hall, *Youth: Its Education, Regimen and Hygiene* (London and New York: Appleton, 1921).

14. Max Kaplan, "New Concepts of Leisure Today," *Journal of Health, Physical Education and Recreation* 43 (March, 1972): 43-46.

15. Konrad Lorenz, "The Enmity Between Generations and Its Probable Ethological Causes," in Marcia W. Piers, Ed., *Play and Development* (New York: W. W. Norton and Company, Inc., 1972).

16. Joyce McLellan, *The Question of Play* (London: Pergamon Press, Ltd., 1970).

17. Maria Montessori, *The Montessori Method,* (New York: Bentley, 1964).

18. Eveline B. Omwake, "The Child's Estate," in Millie Almy, *Early Childhood Play: Selected Readings Related To Cognition and Motivation* (New York: Simon and Schuster, 1968).

19. Dennis K. Orthner, "Leisure Styles and Family Styles: The Need For Integration," *Journal of Health, Physical Education and Recreation* 45 (November/December, 1974): 43-45

20. Eleanor Pavenstedt, Ed., *The Drifters: Children of Disorganized Lower Class Families* (Boston: Little, Brown, 1967).

21. Jean Piaget, *Play, Dreams, and Imitation In Childhood* (London: William Neinemann Ltd., 1951).

22. Sara Smilansky, *The Effects of Sociodramatic Play On Disadvantaged Preschool Children* (New York: John Wiley and Sons, Inc., 1968).

23. Brian Sutton-Smith, "A Syntax for Play and Games," in R. E. Herron and Brian Sutton-Smith, Eds., *Child's Play* (New York: John Wiley and Sons, Inc., 1971).

24. Gregory P. Stone, "American Sports: Play and Display," in Eric Larrabee and Rolf Meyersohn, Eds., *Mass Leisure* (Glencoe, Illinois: The Free Press, 1958).

CHAPTER
TWO

Infants use their mouths actively for exploring and for making sounds.

Development of and through Play

Two basic ideas are presented in this chapter. First, that infants' and young children's play develops in a particular order, and second, that children develop through play. The first part of the chapter describes the order in which particular forms of play appear during development, and, the second part of the chapter examines how play advances children's development in certain areas. This chapter also looks at those areas of development which play usually does not affect.

An understanding of these two basic ideas will help you to benefit from the special strengths of this book. Such an understanding can lead you (a) to observe how individual children play, (b) to consider what children's play tells about their developmental needs and readiness to learn, and (c) to help children use play to promote development. These ideas suggest that you can have an active role in promoting development through play, as indeed you can.

Development

It is no exaggeration to say that play develops in a particular order. Most observers of play generally agree on the order. We will first outline this order briefly, and then fill it in with samples of play that are typical at particular developmental levels. Although we examine play in terms of the ages when particular forms of play are abundant, the overall order is as important as the child's age.

In what order then, does play develop? Play development parallels the general order for all other early development. These two are parallel, we believe, because young children's play is a major way—perhaps *the* major way—of making new experiences a permanent and comfortable part of the self. Therefore, it is helpful to think of play as development.

Before we examine the parallels of play and other development, we must guard against a confusion that often arises when we talk of a developmental order. When we say that a play form abounds at a particular age level, we mean that it typically stands out from other forms of play at that level. But we do not mean to imply that it replaces or conceals all other forms of play. To abound, it need not be present more than all other forms of play combined. With nearly all children, we see a mixture of play forms. From this, we can conclude that the different forms of developmental play overlap. One form does not cease when another becomes more frequent. So, in looking at the outline of play development, we should remember that a typical form of abundant play tends to exceed each of the other forms at a particular age level. Therefore, we say it abounds.

Play as Development. The development of play parallels other development in three major areas. First, play feeds on and into children's physical or motor development. Gesell's work provides a useful description of the developmental order for this area of play. We have updated it with more recent work to construct our outline of the development of motoric play.

Secondly, play development also parallels social development. *Social development* refers to the emergence of a child's overall ability to deal with social reality. *Social reality* means the child in relation to self and to others. Erikson's theory, among others, is the basis for the outline that we use for the development of social play.

Finally, play feeds on and into the child's overall ability to deal with physical reality. We will refer, in this text, to changes in this overall ability as *cognitive development*. Piaget and Smilansky's notions of play along with some more recent studies have been used in our outline of play's development as it relates to cognitive development.

This does not mean that you will need to concern yourself with three different outlines of play. Because you will probably find a single outline more helpful in your work with children, we have compressed these three areas into one outline. In the sense that early childhood development is roughly parallel in the three areas—motoric, social, and cognitive—it is acceptable to construct a single outline to deal with them. Single outlines have been formed in the past by play theorists, but only because theorists tried to relate play to primarily one aspect of development.

However, many individual children show variations in development that further split the rough parallels of motoric, social and cognitive development. Thus, the parallels are present, but more for children in general than for individual children. For this reason, when using a single outline, you will want to remember that the individual child's play development will often deviate from the outline. The overall construct could hold up only if all three major developmental areas were perfectly correlated. But, they are not.

Without taking exceptional or handicapped children into consideration, you can probably remember examples of children whose development was somewhat delayed or advanced in one of these areas. Thinking along these lines will enable you to use this play outline sensibly to understand individual children. That is, consult the outline only after asking yourself if the child's development is even or uneven across the three areas. If it is even, just use the outline. If it is uneven, expect that the outline descriptions which relate to social development, for example, may be ahead of or behind the rest of the outline.

An Outline of Play Development

Play's development can be divided into four stages: sensorimotor play, productive play, reproductive play, and games with rules. Each of these stages is described in this section and, if necessary, contrasted with the other stages. Justifications are given for the names assigned to each stage.

Sensorimotor Play. Sensorimotor play is the earliest form of play. It appears in infancy and is typically prominent until about age two. The word *sensory* emphasizes the roles of (*a*) sucking and mouthing, (*b*) making sounds and listening, and (*c*) gazing at and following moving objects visually, including one's own hands and feet. The word *motor* emphasizes those simple movements of infancy which result in (*a*) control of grasping and handling objects, (*b*) physical mobility from sitting up to eventual walking and running, (*c*) production of speech sounds and the formation of words, and (*d*) exploration and knowledge of one's own body. Play in this period of life is accordingly referred to as *sensorimotor play.*

Some of the characteristic and recognizable activities which, together, make up sensorimotor play are engaging in simple muscular activities, repeating actions and imitating them, trying new actions, imitating and repeating them, and becoming familiar with one's own body by exploration. Infants make sounds and play at repeating and imitating them, and eventually they imitate the sounds and actions of others. Their mouths are used actively both for exploring and for making sounds. These simple forms of play allow them to practice and learn their motor capabilities and to explore and experience their immediate environment. These examples also illustrate why play at this stage is sometimes called *practice play*. That is, children engage in repetitious actions as if these had their own ends without reference to any resulting recognizable outcome. Adults often fail to recognize these early activities as play, because they do not involve the child in the use of traditional play materials.

Productive Play. From about two to four years of age, children learn the uses of simple or manageable play materials, and use them to satisfy their own purposes. That is, they no longer spend so much time repeating actions. Instead, they use materials in ways that most adults would recognize as play, although adults may find the play to be difficult to follow unless it is viewed from the child's own subjective viewpoint. Play at this level is used for the child's own ends rather than as a means of accomplishing some result which adults could recognize as a play outcome. Nevertheless, as children become more skillful in playing with materials, they do begin to produce or construct things. But their play now assimilates the reality of particular materials to their own purposes. The materials and actions are, therefore, not restricted either by conventional standards of performance or of outcome. That is, what children produce is done to satisfy the requirements of their play rather than to match some standard of external reality. In recognition of this change from repetitive play to recognizable play with materials, which produces those results which the child intends, it will be called *productive play*. The word *productive* not only describes such play, but clarifies how it differs from the play of the next stage, which we will call *reproductive*.

We see productive play when children begin to use simple play materials. Eventually they create and construct things, playing longer and concentrating longer. They rough out themes around which to organize their play. Their growing use of language is one reason for these new abilities. Children who achieve at this point self-set play goals are better able to adapt to play goals set by others later.

During these years and in this order, children can and may carefully observe someone else constructing, work at constructing alone, play at constructing next to another child without interacting, play next to another child while observing him from time to time, and (some children) play interactively at constructing things with one or two other children.

Although the social progression we have just described is observed during productive play, children who are very active physically may develop more early contacts with other children unrelated to productive play. Children who are highly curious about the physical world may display a fairly mature pattern of solitary productive playing, although their social development is not necessarily delayed in other respects.

Reproductive Play. A third recognizable form of play is prominent between four and seven years of age. Children progressively use play materials and perform actions in more conventional ways, thereby accomplishing ends that are regulated either by physical reality or by cultural prescription. That is, in contrast to the play of the preceding age period, which is productive of whatever children wish or intend, the play of this period is increasingly reproductive of what they understand about both the physical and social realms of experience. It follows, then, that such standards are not necessarily imposed on them by adults. Rather, both the standards and the desire to accommodate to them evolve along with the child's sharpening comprehension of reality. We are inclined on these grounds to call this the period of *reproductive play*. For reasons that will become evident, we shall also refer to this period with the terms *dramatic play* and *sociodramatic play*.

Productive play develops first but becomes speedier and more efficient toward the end of this stage, when many children will work creatively along with one or two other children. Increased productive skills and increased social contact lead to an increase in the child's potential for reproducing the social realities experienced. This happens especially when children use their imaginations to play different social roles. They imagine and take turns saying and doing what they believe adults might say and do when carrying out adult roles. Through role playing, children learn to take turns and to limit themselves to what is allowed by a particular role. Once they have learned to take turns and to limit their behavior to a set of rules, they can play simple games with rules. Thus, simple game forms appear which become increasingly important at the next age level.

Children, even those who play alone, may move on to social role play using dolls, cars, blocks, and other materials. This is called *dramatic play*. If another child is involved, it is called *sociodramatic* (social dramatic) *play*. So, whether alone or in the company of others, children play to reproduce the social realities of adults.

Children respond to their heightened grasp of physical reality by trying to make what they build, paint, mold, and draw look like the physical realm as they understand it. In fact, at this stage, some children temporarily demonstrate a grasp of physical reality that is so much at odds with their ability to reproduce it, that they become frustrated. They give up, or even actively avoid engaging in those particular accommodative activities.

Games with Rules. The next period extends from about seven to twelve years of age. Games based on rules increase in importance in the early elementary years of this period and decrease in importance in the late elementary years. Dramatic and sociodramatic play continue to be important at this stage, despite school programs which make little provision for them. Making and accepting rules are now reoccurring themes in the child's play. The emphasis on accommodating to rules represents an advance in comprehension over the last stage, when social reality was understood in terms of overt actions and simple, observable roles only. In line with these developments, we call this the period of *games with rules.*

Games with rules have significant consequences for education. The emphasis on rules forces children to cope with their own desires, such as winning, to the extent that these may conflict with their desire to be liked and accepted by their peers. Focusing on rules also leads children to reflect on rules and to ask questions about them. They may discover that they are capable of creating rules themselves, but that once the rules have been adopted they also are bound by them. All of these experiences can help children to understand that, although social agreements or rules may be arbitrarily created, social agreements are binding so long as the game continues.

Illustrations of Play Development

We have just named, described, and contrasted four developmental periods of play, sensorimotor or practice play, productive play, reproductive play, and games with rules. You can understand these better after you study the play sketches below, which illustrate what play is like within each of the stages. As you study the play sketches, you will find it useful to keep in mind the preceding descriptions of and contrasts among the four play stages. For instance, in your study of Roddy, reflect on how he fits the description of sensorimotor play in terms of his specific behaviors.

Sensorimotor Play. Roddy was the first child of a younger couple. Although they were inexperienced parents, they were loving and attentive and enjoyed watching him. His parents report that when Roddy was a baby he would lie in his crib studying the moving shadows on his bedroom wall, then reach out in the direction of the shadows and make happy, gurgling sounds. (Many of Roddy's noises resembled familiar speech sounds, and these he would repeat as if he recognized them and wanted to hear them again.)

One day, as Roddy lay on his back, he held a bright jar lid tightly out in front of him and excitedly waved both arms. He flexed his wrist back and forth examining the lid from different angles, then put it into his mouth. He pushed the lid part way in then held it there while alternately mouthing the lid and gurgling.

When Roddy's parents changed his diaper, they often left him on his back to play before dressing him, at which point he would kick and wave his arms. If his parents talked to him or touched him, he would get very excited and move all his limbs vigorously, kicking his legs in a manner resembling a walking motion.

When Roddy got hungry, he would suck so actively that he would pant for breath. When he was partly satisfied, he would slow down and stop for several seconds and look up at whoever was feeding him. Leaving the nipple partly in his mouth and sucking occasionally, he seemed to enjoy these leisure moments. His moods would vary, from seriously and intently inspecting his parent's face to playfully smiling. This he would interrupt with short bursts of sucking.

His daily bath provided an opportunity for interactive play. He would kick and splash in the water, squint, and make faces. He wanted to hold the wash cloth, squeeze it with both hands, and wave it about overhead. As he grew older he insisted upon having certain favorite toys in the bath with him. The bath itself was a ritual, and every detail had to be correct—proper water temperature, foaming bubble bath, and toys. He usually did not like to have bath time stop.

After Roddy started walking, his parents wanted him to keep his shoes on most of the time. But the more they insisted, the more he seemed to slip out of them. He really seemed to miss his feet when they were inside his shoes and just had to recover them. Once he got the shoes off, he would run around delightedly in barefooted circles enjoying the direct physical contact between feet and floor. These actions reminded his parents of how much he seemed to enjoy his feet in infancy. He used to lie on his back, bring his feet and face together, and pop in a mouthful of toes. He would continue such activity for several minutes.

Whenever he was placed somewhere without toys, Roddy would get very interested in his body. For instance, to help him concentrate during toilet training, his parents did not allow him to have any toys. So he took this opportunity to examine all of the accessible parts of his body. Some of his exploration was so rough that he left parts of himself reddened and temporarily swollen. By that time Roddy was allowed to be in the kitchen so he could be supervised while his parents were preparing the meal. One bottom section of the cupboard had been set aside for him. It was equipped with old pots, pans, measuring spoons, and empty food cartons. Occasionally dolls, blocks, and other toys got mixed in with the kitchen toys. As he banged the pots together, Roddy would stop briefly to reflect on the noise. At other times, he would repeatedly place one small pan inside a larger one and remove it again, occasionally distracted by the noise. He tried for a long time to place the larger pan inside the smaller one until he had thoroughly assured himself that the other combination was more workable. He would stack containers until they fell and then start over again. He would place one hand inside an empty food carton, peer into it and then stuff a rag doll or some blocks inside. This play would continue as long as an adult remained in the kitchen. From time to time, Roddy talked to his parent about what was happening or made some simple request with words and gestures.

Roddy still sat in a high chair at meals, but he was now feeding himself with a spoon and holding his own cup. Mealtime was a social time, and Roddy soon learned that he could get attention and amused responses by clowning. As his language skills increased, however, he entered more easily into the conversation by requesting something or commenting on the food. If his parents talked about him, he leaned forward, beamed, and clasped his hands together while listening. A favorite mealtime game was dropping his spoon on the floor and having someone return it. Adults always tired of this game before Roddy.

Productive Play. Sarah, the youngest of three sisters, enjoyed playing with the others when she was a toddler. By the time she was two and one-half years old, her social interests were, therefore, a little advanced. She enjoyed being around other children and approached children her age fondly. She would pat or embrace them and invite them to play with her. During play, however, she would sit beside a companion without really interacting. She seemed to enjoy having someone nearby. She would occasionally show something to her companion or exhibit curiosity about what the other child was doing.

Sarah was better able than most children her age to take turns. She would allow her companion to hold one of her playthings for a few minutes, and when she thought she had shared the toy long enough, she would tell the other child in a very mature, authoritative way that it was now time for her to have her toy back: "You should let me have it now. It's mine and it's my turn."

Because of Sarah's more mature social outlook, she spent less time clinging tenaciously to toys and more time playing with them. She would pedal her small tricycle a short distance trying to steer with one hand while she clutched a toy truck in the other. She would make motor noises, then suddenly she would dismount and go off running after a bird or a grasshopper, still holding onto the truck. If her chase carried her into a quiet grassy area or flower bed, she sometimes began pushing the truck around and making the motor noise again.

When Sarah's older siblings were away at school, she would play with their toys as well as her own. She would load blocks into the back of the truck and push it around, then unload and reload it. She tried to stack so many blocks on the truck that some would fall off. She would say to herself, "Too many blocks," as if repeating someone else's words. But, she paid no heed to this remark and continued to stack the blocks on the truck.

Her older sisters had some interlocking blocks that they used to construct realistic houses, schools, and hospitals. Sarah, too, made a house with the blocks, although it was more an add-on tower than anything else. "This is my house," she would assert convincingly. She held the blocks close to her face, pressing them together, and observing the small details that permitted her to link them together. She always parked a car or a truck next to the house. She would place a toy log or a stick by the side of the car away from the house and refer to the enclosed space as the carport. She was unconcerned by the fact that the house and carport only minimally resembled real ones. The action of building seemed to be what mattered.

Sarah liked to have her oldest sister or an adult read her favorite stories to her over and over again. When her grandparents visited, she offered to "read" a story to them. Sitting beside her listener, she would turn the pages, and repeat almost exactly the words of the story. She pretended sometimes to be one of the animals or other characters, and she would perform some of the actions from the story. But she would soon slip out of that role and do something else.

She had a favorite toy bear which she played with so much that it was worn and soiled. She would talk to Teddy as if to involve him in her daily routines: "You must wash your hands at once. It's time for lunch." "Come on, Teddy! You know it's time for bed." "Hurry up, Teddy. We're going to the store." Then she would carry out for Teddy the required acts of preparation.

When Sarah was about three and one-half years old, her second sister started to kindergarten. Sarah's parents noticed how alone she felt when both sisters were away. She hardly seemed to know what to do with herself. So they arranged for her to be in a preschool program three mornings a week. At the program center, Sarah seemed to be one of the most advanced among the three year olds and was a leader among her classmates.

Sarah found many activities to occupy her time at the preschool. She worked simple puzzles, made patterns at a pegboard, painted, began to play house and school, strung beads, played tag, and built castles and roads in the sandbox. She was beginning to express some concern that her paintings and drawings did not turn out quite the way she intended. Overall, she showed many play behaviors typical of the reproductive period even before her fourth birthday.

Reproductive Play. When Mark and Tammy were preschoolers, they attended the same day care center until they were old enough to enter kindergarten. Both children were described by their parents as "very busy" and interested in doing new things.

Mark and Tammy had two regular playmates in the day care center, Bob and Larry, who were similarly inclined to be busy. Indoors, they often seemed to think up things to do that disrupted the planned routine. Because the four were all close to the same age, the adult leaders thought they must be going through some kind of phase. For example, when the adults wanted all the children to sit and listen to a story, one of the four, predictably, moved near the storyteller to take a closer look at the pages or to help turn them. At that moment, Mark might raise his hand or just start talking, because something in the story reminded him of an experience that he wanted to relate. About that time, Tammy would turn to one of the other children and begin to elaborate on what Mark was saying. Usually the adult had to stand up and speak loudly to recapture the children's attention.

This happened whenever the adult leader tried to have the children sit and listen. However, when Mark, Tammy, and crew were together outdoors, the outcome was different. They entertained themselves very well by playing hide-and-seek or other simple games. If the adult tried to organize a group game, Tammy and Mark seemed to have no difficulty paying attention or following rules. Further, if the adult was busy taking care of some problem in the play area, Tammy might begin quietly examining a flower, slowly picking off the petals and saying, "One for you and one for me." About then, Mark might suggest, "I know. Let's put some flowers in here," and hold up a discarded container. The two children would then busy themselves collecting dandelions.

Because Tammy and Mark lived in the same neighborhood, their parents often took turns dropping them off at the day care center and bringing them home at night. For this reason, the two children frequently had a chance to play together before and after their program day. At these times, they would pretend to be at the day care center: "You be the child. I'll be the teacher. See, I'm telling you a story." "I don't want a story. I want to play." "No! It's time for our story." "I don't want to be the child." "But you have to be the child." "Can I help with the story?" "O.K. You can help. But when I say 'Quiet,' you have to be quiet."

At other times they would pretend to be parents, or a superhero, or grandma or another visitor talking with them or their parents. Their dramatic play reflected their perceptions of people and events as when they pretended to be teacher and child. But their play reflected more than their perceptions, it revealed their efforts to understand and cope with the often confusing and troubling events of their everyday lives.

Eventually Mark and Tammy were old enough for kindergarten. This was a half-day session in the morning. After school, someone from the day care center met and took them to the center for the rest of the day.

In kindergarten, the program was different than at the day care center. There were still some group activities, but the room was divided into several areas, so the children could choose with which individual activity they wanted to be involved. When they tired of one thing, they could try another.

Mark and Tammy fit well into this program. Now they could continue their dramatic play and games at school. In fact, their teacher encouraged them and urged them to include some of the less active children in their play. Tammy and Mark usually took turns assigning roles to each other and to the children who joined them in the playhouse area. There were even adult clothes to use to play dress-up.

Both of the children were curious about the new things in the science area. Mark brought in some rocks that he had found and inspected them repeatedly with a magnifying glass. "See, these have little holes all over," he remarked. "But you can only see with this," he said, gesturing with the magnifying glass. Tammy observed the fish in the aquarium. She noticed that some of the larger fish kept chasing the smaller fish and biting them. It worried her that none of the fish ever acted like police to put a stop to this. She asked the teacher thoughtfully, "Who makes the fish mind, so they won't hurt the littler ones?" Later the teacher noticed that Tammy pretended to be a large fish which protected the smaller ones. Tammy would say, "You stop that, you old fish! I'm gonna put you in jail if you bite him again." At this challenge, one of her friends would make a fierce face and lunge repeatedly at another child, "I'll eat you, you little fish." "Help, he's eating me," the third child would plead pretending to hide behind Tammy.

Mark saw a television film about a shipwreck. His mother mentioned to the teacher the next morning that he had had trouble going to sleep. He seemed very excited and kept telling her what had happened in the movie, relating every detail of the shipwreck and the survivors' struggles. That morning, Mark went straight to the large block area and began constructing a ship. He put Tammy and two other children to work following his plan. When they had finished, the blocks formed something actually resembling a boat. The children got into the ship, "Close up the boat. There's a bad storm. We'll all crash. Pretend you fall in the water. Then you say, 'Help, I'm drowning!' " "Help, I'm drowning!" "Wait, we'll save you. Just grab this rope." The loud sounds of the drama attracted the attention of nearly everyone in the room. When some of the children crowded in too close to the action, they were told, "Stay back. This is our boat." "You can't come in here."

Games with Rules. Karla was nine years old when her friend Evelyn moved into the same apartment building. The apartments were part of a project financed by the city to provide low-income families with housing they could afford. This building and the one opposite it shared a central outdoor area that was planted like a small park, providing facilities for organized sports activities. Although Karla had one older sister, Tina, who shared a bedroom with her, Karla was so much younger that they did not play together or have the same friends.

Evelyn was the first close friend Karla had. Before Evelyn came to the building, Karla spent much of her after-school hours alone in the apartment reading or listening to music on the radio. Each morning her mother left instructions for preparing supper. Tina would come in from whatever she was doing at about the same time each evening and start preparing the meal. Karla was to help Tina, but Tina usually didn't ask her to help until the food was cooking. Then Karla stayed in the kitchen to make sure nothing burned or boiled over, while Tina washed the dishes from breakfast and the previous evening. Their mother usually got home from work about that time and they ate together.

After Evelyn moved in, Karla would invite her over after school, and sometimes they would go down into the play area. Usually they could not go to Evelyn's apartment because her father was a shift worker who slept days. Karla and Evelyn talked a lot about what happened at school. They discussed their friendship and how important it was to them. Evelyn told Karla about how frequently her family had moved in the past from place to place. She hoped, now that she had met Karla, that they would not move again. The girls made plans about what they would do if either of them had to move away: "I'll call you up every day after school." "Maybe I could stay at your apartment overnight sometimes."

Both girls collected comic magazines. They did not like comics about crime and war. They liked the ones about animated, silly characters—either animal or human—and these comics they shared back and forth. This became a problem whenever either girl decided at night that she wanted to look at a comic which she had loaned to her friend, because neither girl's parents liked the idea of their going to the other's apartment after supper. So the girls would talk to each other over the phone instead, and one might even read to the other from a comic which the latter had forgotten to take home. Or they discussed what was on the radio or television.

Both girls had some dolls. At times, they played with baby dolls, although they often enjoyed grown-up dolls which they could dress in special outfits. "Tina has an outfit just like this." "They have a bride outfit for my doll. I saw it on TV. Mother says she'll help me make one out of some lace that she saved." "Let's dress up like we're going to a wedding." While dressing: "I wonder what it's like to get married. Did you ever see a wedding?" The girls would stand in front of the mirror viewing themselves. "After you get dressed you put on lots of lipstick. Then you have to march all the way to the front of the church." "What if you tripped?" "You couldn't trip because you're holding onto your father's arm." "I looked at Tina's magazines about dating and stuff, but they don't have any pictures."

Karla and Evelyn enjoyed playing various table games. An uncle had taught Evelyn to play rummy. One day she offered to teach her friend: "Karla, it's lots of fun. I'll show you how to play. See, first you mix up the cards like this. Now you have to cut the cards." "Why do we do that?" "It's just how you do it. Then I deal seven cards like this. Now we're ready to play. You're first." "What am I supposed to do now?" Their conversations about new games were often like this. They tended to focus on the specific steps required in play without identifying the purposes and strategies involved.

Both girls showed some concerns about the outcome of such games. "Are we practicing or does the score count?" Even when a game had been declared as practice in advance, the girl who won wanted to claim the victory, the other maintaining that the score didn't count that time.

Karla knew how to play a guessing game. First you thought of a word and stated only how many letters it had. The other person had to guess the word by asking, one at a time, if it had a particular letter in it. If your partner made a correct guess, you had to write down the letter, showing its actual position within the word. But if the letter guessed wasn't in the word, it was a point against the guesser. The version of the game that Karla knew was called "hangman." After each wrong guess another part of the guesser's body was drawn on a gallows until head, body, arms, legs, hands, and feet were all showing. The loser was now declared "hanged." The girls would play this game for as long as an hour at times, each keeping score of how many times the other had been hanged.

Evelyn liked to play "dodge ball" and "hopscotch" as well as "statues" (or "freeze" as some children call it). After Evelyn moved to the building, Karla went downstairs more often to play some of these games. Karla did not like dodge ball because she could never seem to avoid getting hit. But she soon could play hopscotch as well as Evelyn. Other children joined them at hopscotch. The girls kept close track of their wins to see who would be the champion of the whole apartment building. Playing statues provided for a different kind of competition. Although there were usually no winners or losers declared, the child who could strike the most original, interesting or humorous pose would succeed in gaining admiring or amused reactions from the other children. The game also allowed the children to let themselves go and to be and feel as silly as they wished.

The girls observed other kinds of play taking place in the park area. Many children played games in which the opposing sides "fought" one another to control territory, or so that the good forces would win over the bad forces. Neither Karla nor Evelyn cared for such games, although they sometimes watched with fascination. When they were alone, they would remark that those games were no fun because all you did was pretend to injure someone or to be injured. Their parents didn't approve of such play even though most of the other parents did not care or thought it was harmless.

At school, one teacher helped organize the children's play during recesses and after lunch. Karla and Evelyn looked forward to playing kick ball at these times. Two children would be captains and choose sides. If either Karla or Evelyn was chosen first, they would both plead to have the other one picked by the same side. The team captains usually obliged them. The girls would get very emotionally involved in the play, feeling elated if their team was winning and feeling dejected if they were losing. They formed their own opinions of whether the referee made correct calls and applications of the rules. The events and outcomes of these daily games were often a subject of their after school discussions. They would speculate about whose side they might be on the following day and who would win.

Once when Evelyn's parents both had to go away for the night, Evelyn persuaded them to ask Karla's mother if she might stay overnight with Karla. This was arranged by having Tina stay in her mother's room so Evelyn could have her place. That night the girls had trouble getting to sleep. They kept thinking of things to talk about. The longer they talked, the more humorous everything seemed to become. The following morning Evelyn remarked, "Don't you wish we were sisters so I'd never have to leave." "Let's pretend that we're twin sisters, but not the kind that look exactly alike." "That's a good idea, Sis! Let's go see what Mom is fixing for breakfast."

Development through Play

Many recent articles and some books tend to exaggerate or distort the contributions of play to children's development. Generally, this distortion is a result of an enthusiastic belief in the value of play and stems from the desire of some writers to encourage others to rediscover play. Although this is a commendable objective, their means of achieving it are not easily justified. Distorted ideas of what play can accomplish do not in the long run serve the best interests of children or of early childhood practice. In this section, "Development through Play," we try to bring a realistic perspective into play's contribution to development throughout early childhood.

If other writers tend to distort the importance of play to early development, you might wonder how it would be possible for us to correct this. We have gone about it by using both (a) new information and (b) a different point of view.

Our new information comes from a special review of research and practitioner literature on children's play from three through five years of age.[1] For purposes of this discussion, the information from the literature was very helpful, but it did not cover the ages from birth to three or from six to eight. We needed, therefore, information that would give us a perspective to apply to both infancy and the primary years.

The proposition which we used is that child development is progressive and sequential, with different competencies developing at each stage. We have inferred several corollaries from this viewpoint. First, that play contributes to the development of different competencies at each stage. Further, because play contributes to these competencies, it follows that it contributes less to the development of some other competencies at particular stages.

These two positions are in fact supported by a study which forms one basis for our view.[2] We have included a table from that study (Table 1) to illustrate the point that play seems to contribute more to a particular aspect of development at a particular developmental age than to other aspects. For example, at three years of age, "sorting or grouping" (competency 5) appears to be a high activity learning area, whereas "perceiving from parts" (competency 15) is a low activity area. The full names of these competencies appear in Appendix A.

The table also shows, that for particular competencies, play may contribute much to development at one stage and little at another. For example, play contributes much to "social uses of language" (competency 17) at three years of age but little to this at five years of age.

Table 1

Play Study Results Related to Competencies and Ages

Competency	Developmental Ages		
	3	4	5
1 Forming concepts	L	M	M
2 Sound discrimination	M	L	L
3 Sight discrimination	H	H	H

H = high importance
M = medium importance
L = low importance

Competency	Developmental Ages		
	3	4	5
4 Touch discrimination	M	M	M
5 Sorting or grouping	H	M	M
6 Ordinating	M	M	M
7 Conserving	L	L	L
8 Measuring	L	L	M
9 Perceiving spatial relations	L	M	M
10 Judging causation	H	M	M
11 Recognizing time	L	L	L
12 Other nature concepts	L	M	M
13 Using imagination	H	H	H
14 Adding, subtracting	L	M	M
15 Perceiving from parts	L	M	M
16 Remembering	M	M	M
17 Social uses of language	H	M	L
18 Labeling	M	L	L
19 Explaining	M	M	M
20 Describing	M	M	M
21 Articulating	M	M	L
22 Expressing feelings	M	M	L
23 Using non-verbal cues	M	L	L
24 Comprehending	L	L	L
25 Using typical sentences	M	L	L
26 Asking questions	M	M	M
27 Using "private speech"	H	M	L
28 Recognizing emotions	L	L	L
29 Constructing	H	H	H
30 Copying	M	M	H
31 Drawing	M	M	M
32 Expressing feelings bodily	M	M	L
33 Controlling large muscles	H	M	M
34 Controlling small muscles (not 29-31)	M	M	M
35 Initiating action; showing curiosity	H	H	H
36 Planning action; anticipating	M	H	L
37 Persisting in action	M	M	H
38 Being self-reliant; self-help	H	L	M
39 Sustaining health and safety	L	L	L
40 Trying, accepting new things	L	L	L
41 Waiting a short time	L	L	L
42 Accepting some rules	L	L	L
43 Having preferences	H	H	H
44 Releasing tensions	M	M	L
45 Showing courtesy	M	M	M
46 Following adult directions	M	M	M
47 Responding to social reinforcers	M	M	M
48 Assuming positive social behaviors	M	M	M
49 Getting attention (of others)	M	M	M
50 Maintaining attention (of others)	M	M	M
51 Role playing	H	H	L

	Competency	Developmental Ages		
		3	4	5
52	Respecting others	M	M	M
53	Imitating adults	H	H	L
54	Having a friend	M	H	H
55	Feeling secure with adults	M	M	M
56	Understanding place in family	M	M	L
57	Understanding self	M	M	M
58	Asserting rights	M	M	L
*(59)				

*Appalachia Educational Laboratory later added one more competency to the list, which was not included in this study.

Moreover, the existence of the four developmental stages of play described earlier in this chapter tends to reinforce this perspective. That is, different forms of play abound or predominate at each stage, suggesting that the different emerging competencies of each period call for different kinds of play to support their development.

A point to be considered is: Play does not contribute equally to all aspects of development. This is contrary to the widely held position that play contributes equally to all aspects of development. Further, we conclude that our viewpoint is developmental. A more complete statement of this view is—play does not contribute equally to all aspects of development at any particular age. We are, on the other hand, inclined to believe that play contributes heavily to all aspects of child competency development *at some time* during the years of early childhood.

The preceding discussion is not simply a matter of being more accurate. It is, instead, a point of view which has practical implications that are developed throughout the balance of this text. These implications may be illustrated by referring to educators who tend to overgeneralize the benefits of play. They also tend to ignore the issue of how adults can relate to or provide for children's specific play needs. We suggest that adults should provide primarily for those forms of play which, in consideration of the child's developmental level and needs, will contribute most to those competencies which are currently emerging.

If we review the stages of play in the context of what is known about development at various levels throughout early childhood,[3] we reach the following four stage-related conclusions.

Sensorimotor play contributes in the first two years of life to the development of

(a) the use of senses to acquire basic information
(b) attachment to parenting figures and development of familiarity with the immediate environment
(c) basic postural control and physical mobility

(d) a core sense of the self as a source of desire, intention, and action
(e) hand-eye coordination
(f) a tendency to explore the immediate environment and to experiment physically with objects
(g) acquisition of speech and simple language
(h) ability to name objects
(i) memory.

Productive play contributes to the development of

(a) autonomy, personal preferences, and ability to be assertive
(b) sensory discrimination in relation to broad attributes of objects (e.g., color, form, size, loudness)
(c) ability to sort or group objects according to their broad physical attributes
(d) use of a more social form of language in relating and expressing personal ideas and feelings
(e) fine motor control in conjunction with planning and construction
(f) self-help skills
(g) imitative ability and early forms of role playing
(h) understanding the self in relation to others in the family
(i) imagination
(j) social initiative
(k) more sure-footed, less accident-prone physical mobility.

Reproductive play contributes to the development of

(a) visual discrimination of finer details, and use of touch to guide visual exploration
(b) perceiving whole objects from their parts
(c) perceiving relative positions of objects in space
(d) practical (intuitive) concepts
(e) ability to ordinate, add, and subtract small numbers
(f) use of language to sustain private and social activities and to release tensions
(g) active memory strategies
(h) increased inhibition of action or choice while pondering alternatives
(i) imitative construction
(j) increased attention, task persistence, and directed curiosity
(k) more mature forms of attention-getting
(l) simple understanding of natural phenomena.

The games with rules period contributes to development of

(a) sustained adaptation to routine
(b) conservation, concepts proper, and ability to measure and tell time

(c) formal academic skills

(d) ability to shift perspective

(e) refined fine motor skills (e.g., drawing, writing, and use of musical instruments)

(f) social problem-solving techniques

(g) more reciprocal relations with peers

(h) total integration of large and fine motor actions

(i) sense of accomplishment

(j) ability to apply rules to particular situations

(k) social graces and courtesies

(l) deeper feeling for others

(m) intersensory integration,

(n) self-initiated activities and pursuits which are better organized and attentive to greater detail.

These descriptions are necessarily general. They tend, therefore, to obscure or omit some important, detailed aspects of development in the interest of demonstrating the overall order. For example, hand-eye coordination is identified as a developmental outcome of sensorimotor play, but in fact, hand-eye coordination continues to develop during each of the remaining three stages of early childhood play. But basic hand-eye coordination develops most rapidly during the stage of sensorimotor play. Thus, the reader should be cautious of the general character of these descriptions. You should be careful not to conclude that a particular aspect of development results from, and only from, play at that particular stage. The descriptions are only a general guide to the behaviors which result from particular play stages.

It is also worth noting that each play stage contributes to many areas of development. This is true partly because, within each stage, not all of these activities evolve simultaneously. Thus, some of the developmental outcomes appear earlier and others later within a stage. For example, in the sensorimotor play stage, the development of the use of senses to acquire basic information begins very early in the period and continues throughout, whereas the development of speech and simple language begins in the second half of the stage. The adult who is planning and providing for a particular child's play should pay attention not only to the child's general play stage characteristics, but also to the particular areas in which development is occurring. That is, you will need to be alert to all emerging aspects of development within the stage, and provide for each one as needed.

Some of the specifics of play for which you will need to make provision within each stage are discussed in the following chapters.

NOTES

1. Edward E. Gotts and Karin Oddsen Taylor, *Children's Activities Study (Play Study).* (Charleston, W. Va.: Appalachia Educational Laboratory, 1975).

2. Edward E. Gotts and Karin Oddsen Taylor, 1975.

3. For example, see: Annie L. Butler, Edward Earl Gotts, and Nancy L. Quisenberry, *Early Childhood Programs: Developmental Objectives and Their Uses.* (Columbus, Ohio: Charles E. Merrill Publishing Company, 1975).

USING PLAY TO PROMOTE DEVELOPMENT

II

Part II describes how play promotes development in the child. These five chapters are directed toward both parents and teachers and toward students preparing to work in classroom and child care settings.

- Chapter Three describes the ways in which the child develops an understanding and mastery of his physical environment.
- Chapter Four describes the development of the social environment through play, which includes communication, interaction and social skills, and impulse behavior.
- Chapter Five describes how the child develops as an individual, including the development of self-identity, body control, uses of the senses, personal preferences, and emotional concerns.
- Chapter Six outlines the development of imagination, fantasy, and recreation and tension release.

Finally

- Chapter Seven provides direction for locating and using materials that facilitate play and discusses the criteria for their selection.

Part II, by exploring these topics, provides specific examples of the ways children play, how they develop through play, and how adults can facilitate and guide play so that maximum value is realized.

CHAPTER

THREE

*Clay, sand, or mud play gives children the
chance to explore how substances change.*

Understanding and Mastering the Physical Environment (a descriptive approach)

In the first two chapters, we discussed the value of play relative to the ideas of educators, psychologists, and learning theorists. We also outlined the stages of play and described how these stages are manifested in children's lives. With such obvious and well-founded reasons, one may wonder why play is not incorporated more often into our educational systems.

In this chapter, we will examine how children come to understand and master their physical environment through play. You will see that some activities predominate at the infant stage of development, others during the preschool years, and still others predominate in the primary years. You will also see that understanding and mastering the physical environment is a cognitive task although some affective and psychomotor skills are involved.

Since much of the discussion in this chapter applies to very young children, and since parents and other adults often give children very general guidance, this chapter is not so explicit as later chapters regarding the adult role in the situations described. Rather, we have sought to describe children's use of play as it relates to incidents in their everyday lives. The following examples will show you how a child responds to various situations. You need to be aware of responses you can make to children in similar situations, and you should make note of the toys, materials, and equipment which were used in the following anecdotes.

Objects That Move and Make Sounds

Almost from birth, children seem intent on learning about their environment. When you watch infants, you can see their interest in the environment. They respond especially to sounds and noises. They look for the origin of the noises and are sometimes frightened by them, though at the same time they are often curious. When the noises are combined with quick, unexpected movements, infants often exhibit a startle reflex which is usually accompanied by crying. The parent or adult with the infant can help to make the experience less disturbing by offering reassurance and comfort.

Very early in the child's life, human voices take on meaning. A soft, melodic voice is very soothing. Often, such a voice can be used to calm a crying or frightened child. A loud, harsh voice is frightening to a child. Most children learn early to recognize a change in the tone of their parents' or teacher's voice and respond accordingly. Sometimes, they seem to be testing the adult to see just how far they can go. An observer often can tell that the child knows when the level of tolerance has been reached and that it is time to stop. An example of this is the child whose mother calls that it is time for dinner. The child continues playing while the mother calls several times more. Suddenly, as though the message has just been given, the child drops everything and rushes into dinner, knowing that some other alternative awaits if there is no response to her last call. Even very young toddlers come to understand this aspect of the human voice.

American children who live in areas where nonstandard English is spoken often become interested in dialectical differences in their classmates' language during kindergarten and first grade. With the advent of busing in many of our cities, teachers and parents have an opportunity to help children increase their awareness and understanding of others who speak differently. Young children are also very curious about people who speak a language different from theirs. Left to their own initiative, they will interact with a foreign-speaking person, learn some of the language, and in a very short time, will be able to converse in the language.

Children are fascinated by animal sounds. Some of the first imitations they try to make are animal sounds, especially dogs, cats, cows, and horses. City children are often limited in the kinds of animals they hear, but television shows and records can provide them with the experience of listening to and identifying animal sounds. Unlike urban children, children in small towns, suburban neighborhoods, and on farms have many opportunities to hear different kinds and sizes of dogs bark. Adults should be careful with preschool children and toddlers that their curiosity, especially for dogs that run loose, does not present a danger to the child. An unhappy, frightening experience with a dog at age three or four can stay with a child for some time.

Another category of sounds that fascinate children is those made by machines. Some machines are in their environment long before they are aware of them. For example, mothers are urged to run the vacuum sweeper even when a newborn infant is asleep so that the baby can become accustomed to such noises. Toddlers and preschoolers are often heard moving and acting like a vacuum sweeper. The sounds of the telephone bell and the door buzzer fascinate children, too. They often are startled by such sounds and try to determine from where the sound is coming. The sound of the telephone is easier to locate than the doorbell or buzzer, unless it is attached to hanging chimes, which are obvious to anyone in the room.

The interest in the telephone and its sounds represents several experiences for the child. At first, there is just the interest in hearing it ring. Then there is the experience of hearing a voice on the phone. For example, Jamey would hear his father's voice or one of his grandparent's voices on the phone, and a very inquisitive look would appear on his face. If his father asked him a question, he would shake his head yes or no but never say anything. Even though he was talking well enough to answer the questions, it was several months before he would actually answer the person on the phone. Even then, his answers were short and not at all conversational like his usual personal speech. Gradually, his ability to converse on the phone increased, although the niceties of polite phone conversation did not appear until around age nine.

The sound of the dishwasher, clothes washer and dryer, mixer, and hair dryer are examples of other machine sounds a child hears in the home. The refrigerator, especially a noisy one, a can opener, or an electric knife will evoke curious stares from an infant, elicit some exploratory behavior on the part of a toddler, and provoke questions from a preschooler. By the time children are in preschool, they want to know why the machine makes a noise, how it works, and what it does. Although they do not want a technical explanation, they do need simple, understandable answers.

The sounds from television, radio, tape recorders or record players are sources of interest to children. Here they can hear voices, animal sounds, machine sounds, and music from a secondary source. Many babies grow accustomed to going to sleep to music before their first birthday. Toddlers and preschoolers will sit in front of a record player and listen alone or with others to their favorite records. Although White's work indicates that children, before the age of three, do not watch more than two minutes of television per waking hour, many young children are around a television that is turned on for many hours. Thus, the television sounds are very much a part of their lives.[1] Four year olds, depending upon parental supervision, generally increase their viewing time. After children enter school, their viewing time is somewhat regulated by the decreased number of hours the television is available.

Once children move outside the home, they find many interesting noises.

Toddlers are fascinated by the lawnmower. Many youngsters have push toys, that make noises like a popcorn popper or a toy lawnmower. Here we see that children are not only interested in the noises, but also in the movement of the machine. Tools which parents use are also fascinating. Electric saws, drills, lathes, or the sound from a hammer will attract attention. Most children soon imitate both the actions and the sounds in their play whether they have the replicas of the tools or not.

Most children learn about cars, trucks, and motorcycles quite early. Engine noise is perhaps not as interesting as the car horn or the sound of the buzzer from an opened door or an unfastened seat belt. It is always amazing to parents to discover how early their baby recognizes their car in the driveway, particularly when the car has an unusual sound in the motor or in the horn. Some parents learn early that an infant who is upset will sleep quickly and easily when driven in a car. Whether this is due to the engine sound or the car motion is debatable; but so far as the parent is concerned, it works.

Children may react differently to the sound of trucks and motorcycles. Initially the infant may be frightened by the volume of the sounds made by the motor. This is especially so when a child is reared on a quiet street or road, and the truck or motorcycle is unusually loud. Toddlers show a great deal of interest in what makes cars, trucks, and motorcycles go. Through preschool, children display curiosity about lights, gear shifts, windshield wipers, and horns. We often see preschoolers imitating these machines both in action and sounds. An extreme example of imitating sounds was Bobby, who called every piece of equipment by its sound. Thus a tractor was a *clank, clank, clank;* the motorcycle was *bummm, bumm, bumm;* the car was *errrr, errrr, errr.* Unfortunately, his parents and older brothers all encouraged his use of sounds to identify objects and never gave him the correct names for such machines.

Trains, airplanes, bulldozers, and graders are a group of machines that are further removed from most children's experience. In fact, the train and the sounds associated with the train often demonstrate the generation gap between parents/grandparents and children. Most adults talk about trains going "choo-choo," while actually there are very few places in present-day America where a child can hear a steam engine. Except for some local uses and for excursions, steam engines have been replaced by diesels. The child who has seen a diesel-powered train can be confused by the parent or adult who suggests that his small wooden train goes "choo-choo, choo-choo."

Trains represent a possible frightening experience for very young children. The noise and speed which accompanies them can be very frightening, and the size of the engine to one who is only two to three feet tall is formidable. Still, there is a fascination in trains which behooves parents and teachers to explore them with their children. One of the most interesting field trips I have ever participated in was a trip with three and four year olds to explore a locomotive in the train yards in Terre Haute, Indiana. The entire class of children climbed aboard the engine accompanied by teachers and parents.

The engineer showed each child how to ring the bell and let each one have a turn as the engine moved slowly out of the round house and down through the train yards. The children were intrigued with the throttle and the levers which the engineer maneuvered. If there were any fears, they were overcome by teachers and parents who held the hands of children who needed support. Needless to say, this group of children was very realistic in their train play following this experience.

Airplanes, especially jets, are even more removed from children's everyday experiences, although families who live close to large airports often take their children to watch airport traffic. Even without this experience, many children are aware of the sound of planes overhead and have watched airplanes on television. They are curious about them and use toy airplanes in their play if they are available. You may want to arrange a field trip so that the children in your class can see a real airplane. Many airports and small airfields have planes available for children to walk through (or climb into if it is a very small plane).

Large equipment and machines become of interest to children as they become aware of them. Here, too, the noise may keep the child from wanting to explore such equipment; and encouragement and support from his parent or another adult may be necessary. Ditch digging equipment, street repair trucks and equipment, bulldozers, tractors, and Caterpillars interest children as they become acquainted with them. Sometimes children notice equipment when there is work going on in front of their house, or a water pipe breaks in the yard and equipment is brought in to repair it. Sometimes they notice a new building going up in the neighborhood or they visit a farm which presents the child with a whole new world of experiences, sounds, and motions.

Sounds from nature, such as thunder, rain, wind, hail, and sleet are all intriguing to the child. A safe, secure place in a parent's arms can introduce the child to phenomena that can be frightening under different circumstances. All parents and many teachers have experienced the wide-eyed, frightened look of a child aroused by the first loud clap of thunder. Observation and discussion are important considerations for alleviating fears about these natural phenomena. Examining hail after a beating hail storm helps the child to understand what it is and how it is formed. Talking about the different sounds the wind makes, listening to it, and talking about why the intensity differs are possible at most levels of understanding through adulthood.

The list of things which interest children through sound and movement is probably endless. But one must also consider the objects and materials in the child's environment that move and make sounds when the child does something to them. All of the things discussed in the preceding pages can be imitated. Toy dolls and animals can be moved to imitate people and animal behaviors. Sounds can be imitated even to the extent of two- and three-way conversations among dolls and animals. This provides valuable learning opportunities for exploring the environment.

Almost as soon as a child can manipulate a toy car, truck, bus, or train, we see an imitation of the real thing. Play moves from simple straightforward movements and sounds to complex, involved, reproductive play. By age four or five this play may include more than one other child. By primary age, imitating machines can be quite involved, with the child playing at and building structures that imitate what he has seen.

Bells, rattles, squeeze toys, etc., interest the very young. At first, they must depend upon their parents or others in their home to reproduce sounds for them; but very early in their lives, they are able to make the sounds themselves. As they become more capable, they move from striking the bells on their cradle gym to squeezing the rubber toys in their playpen. As soon as they can move around and manipulate things by themselves, they play with toys which they must push and pull to make noise. Toddlers delight in pulling a quacking duck, a barking dog, or a clackety-clack train through the house or down the sidewalk. It is important that these kinds of toys be provided for children.

During the preschool years, the child moves to toys and materials that make noise because of some outside action. Some toys, such as sound boards with a telephone dial that rings, a buzzer, or a bicycle bell, provide the child with the opportunity to produce sounds. Other sound toys are wind-up radios or small television-like sets that play a favorite song, like "Pop Goes the Weasel" or "Mary Had a Little Lamb." Musical toys are also interesting to children during this period, such as wind-up stuffed toys and musical tops.

Play materials with moving parts are available, such as a garage with a car elevator and a buzzer announcing the floors. Children can spend hours with such toys. They move from these kinds of play materials to motorized (battery-operated or electric) trains, airplanes, and even small cars. These items are usually found in homes, purchased from the toy store, and not in schools. They are more easily manipulated by the primary age child than the preschooler.

Musical instruments—drums, bells, and tambourines—can be introduced to very young children. Toddlers will try to help anyone playing a piano or an organ and can be taught to treat both with respect. Since rhythm develops fairly early, young children enjoy and can use simple instruments. Guitars are often imitated by youngsters, who love to listen and watch while an adult plays. Dan, a three year old, was such a child. As his uncle fingered the notes on the guitar, he would strum the strings and "play" the song. He would stay with this until his fingers blistered if his uncle was not careful. Another youngster, a four year old in a Head Start Center was observed vigorously tapping his foot and pretending to strum a guitar or banjo. He obviously had someone at home to model for his "playing."

Three and four year olds all over the country are learning to master the violin by following the Suzuki method. Other preschool-age children are mastering drums, xylophones, and rhythm instruments using the Orff-Kodaly method.[2] This interest in instruments merges into concentrated practice and effort by primary age, although the same response, noted in toddlers, can be found in first and second graders when they are exposed to instruments for the first time.

One object of considerable interest to the child is the sound when a toilet is flushed. Of course, other factors enter into the child's interest in the toilet, such as the disappearance of what is in the toilet and especially the splash of water. The wise parent provides other sources for water splashing—which provides a nice sound as well as a good feeling—such as in the bath, at the sink, or in a pan or tub in the yard. Teachers, too, need to provide opportunities to splash water, for with very young children in nursery schools and day care centers, the caregiver often must take the place of the parent in such matters.

Appearance of Things

As Piaget has indicated, children up to about the age of seven have developed only preconcepts. (We will refer to these preconcepts as *concepts,* with the understanding that it is a matter of terminology and not a disagreement with Piaget's theory.) From about age four or five, concepts are formed which help children relate to their environment. By age three children usually have a concept of big and little, and seem to understand adjectives such as *little, small, and big.* Some time later, they can compare the size of two objects, and talk about bigger–biggest, smaller–smallest. They can talk about minor differences and ask for the biggest truck or the biggest cookie. They may talk about one block being bigger than another or one ball being the biggest of all.

By kindergarten, children can vaguely comprehend what a series of little-to-big can be. Children can compare adjacent rods, for example; but when rods are placed in a series, they appear jumbled. This relates to an inability to comprehend the whole set of rods arranged from smallest to biggest. By first grade, children's size-related language has increased greatly. Such words as *large, small, longest, shortest, widest, largest, smallest,* and *tallest* are used. Size can be related to people as well as to objects, toys, and equipment. Throughout this period children need help in describing size. When talking about objects and toys, adults should use terms like *tallest* or *smallest.* It is helpful to ask questions, such as "Which dog is bigger?" or "Which tree is the tallest?"

Children are interested in form and shapes. Clay, sand, and mud give them an opportunity to explore the changes which take place by molding them and give children the opportunity to observe what happens when water is added to these substances. At the earliest levels, children seem to simply explore. They put sand in a tray or pan and then pour it out. They learn that if water is added, sand packs down and does not pour, and the same thing happens with mud. Too much water makes sand or a mud pie runny.

Children can spend many months playing with these objects. Then, gradually, they begin to build structures, tunnels, roads, and even cities. The sand, or wet dirt, takes on more complex forms as they interpret their experiences on a smaller scale. This latter play often involves cars, trucks, other toys, and other children.

The form of natural phenomena also intrigues children. Water changing to ice can be observed on a sidewalk or patio or demonstrated in the refrigerator. Although it is some time before they can understand why snow, sleet, or hail form, they are still interested in and love to play in snow. Many teachers and parents use snow to make ice cream so that children can experience it in yet another form.

You could provide cooking experiences where children see first hand how different foods change form. Preschoolers, as well as older children, also love to make Jello and pudding. You could help them see how a powder dissolves in water and then changes into a solid form. Cooking rice or macaroni shows children how a hard, solid food becomes soft. Cooking and mashing potatoes is another food activity which interests children, especially when they have an opportunity to eat some of the raw potato and then some of the mashed. By keeping some of the raw potatoes aside, the children can compare the raw and the cooked directly. This interest in cooking, and observing changes in food, matures with the child until they begin cooking and baking by themselves around the age of ten.

Color plays a big part in children's lives. It is possible to purchase toys for home use which are color coded. You will hear references to color when they play with these toys. Preschoolers find it rather easy to learn the basic color names. They talk about their blue sweater or red socks. They notice a yellow car or a red fire engine. They make up games matching blocks of the same color or matching other toys by color.

Children are attracted to the way things feel. They like soft, fuzzy, wooly pillows, animals, and blankets. You can often observe a baby feeling the satin on a blanket or rubbing a soft, fuzzy bear. Children compare the feel of different grades of sandpaper. They may even ask why there are such differences and how they are used. Children are sensitive to the feel of dress up clothes, often complaining that something is too scratchy or too hot. It is helpful if parents and adults use adjectives which label what the child is feeling, such as *warm, soft, scratchy.*

Similarities and Differences

Preschoolers begin to understand part/whole relationships when they name or point to parts of their own bodies or those of a doll. They become interested in and are able to assign similar things to classes or groups. They most frequently group by color, size, form, or texture. They can understand the concept of similarity and can tell what objects are alike and what objects are different. They can move beyond identifying or looking at single objects to comparing classes of things.

By late preschool, children can pick out of a group of objects, identify things that do not belong and can sing along with songs that do just that on shows like "Sesame Street." They can even identify partial likenesses and differences. By primary age, objects can be grouped by function. The list of experiences which engage the child in classification activities is endless. Most occur in the area of science or natural phenomena. Observation of animals occurs naturally in a child's life. These observations lead to a natural comparison of how, for example, dogs, cats, hamsters, guinea pigs, and other small animals differ. Many young boys and girls have been observed lying flat on the ground watching an ant or a colony of ants work. After a number of such experiences, they can tell you that black ants are a little different from red ants or brown ants. Children spend hours exploring situations like these.

There is a wide variety of toys that help children to classify and sort. Some require stringing a red necklace; others require setting up a pattern of alternating colors. Blocks often have not only different colors, but also different shapes. Activities like determining what floats or what sinks lead to differentiation. These findings are often overheard in children's attempts to plan dramatic and/or creative play activities.

Preschoolers use games which involve color matching, form matching, animal matching, and many other kinds of matching. Some children make their own matching games, given the materials to work with. A can of buttons, or a set of pots and pans have served many young children well in classification and grouping skills.

Labels or Descriptors

Soon after children learn to talk, they start into a "What's that?" stage. From then on, they seem intent on learning what things are and what they are called. This is the way in which children learn to communicate and interact verbally with others. Without labels for things and adjectives to describe them, children could not function well with others. Bobby, the little boy who was cited earlier as having his own names for things, was a difficult child for other children to play with. Another four year old was observed one day simply walking away from him in frustration. He could not understand what Bobby was talking about and just gave up trying to play with him.

As children play, they talk aloud to themselves almost constantly, both when they are alone and with other children. This talking aloud not only provides language practice, but also provides practice for concept development. For example, a child may have a conversation with trucks or their drivers, or may tell a truck what to do. This monologue, or solitary speech, may include descriptions of the truck, such as the color, the kind, or the company name. Some of this conversation is really the child's reinforcing ideas for himself.

This is especially observable in the housekeeping corner. We very often hear children describe a doll in terms they hear at home. Sometimes, they appear to be using words they wish would be used with them instead of with the baby. Listening for these kinds of remarks and being aware of the feelings behind them is an important part of being a parent or a teacher. Not only do we learn what children know, or how learning develops, but we also learn what they feel.

Since having correct labels and descriptors is so important to the child's cognitive growth, the parent or teacher has a responsibility to respond to the child's play and provide such information. Some of this information you can glean through conversation with the child. Some you can get through games, toys, materials, and activities provided. But even these need your verbal reinforcement, additions, and mind-stretching input if the child's language is to grow into adult language.

The most important activity in the area of language development is hearing good stories read aloud and listening to them on records and tapes. Story ideas are expressed in ways that are very different from everyday conversation. The child will hear unfamiliar words and names for things that are not commonly used. The Beatrix Potter books about Peter Rabbit and his friends are an example of unfamiliar English language usage, because they were written for British children.

The Concept of Time

Time is more meaningful to young children in terms of events rather than minutes, hours, or days. They find it very difficult to wait until after dinner for a special activity or until next week to take a trip to their grandparents. Most parents and teachers wait a day or two before a trip before telling children about it.

You may hear preschoolers refer in their conversation or in their play to the "next morning" or something that happened last night. You may also hear them talking about what they are going to do later in the day or the next day. In a limited way, children relate to time and make plans for different times of the day.

They may show an interest in watches and clocks somewhat early, but the majority of children are still unable to tell time until second or third grade. Even then they are more apt to be able to tell the hour and half-hour than to calculate minutes.

Children preschool age and older often relate events to their own lives. They talk about when they were babies and like to look at pictures of themselves, especially movie films of their first eighteen months. They put events into a time frame relative to when they lived in a certain house or apartment, particularly if the family has moved often.

The child talks about things from the past using past tense. He can also talk about things in the future, such as "He'll go there" or "He'll be there tomorrow." This usage becomes more exact as the child approaches school age. The child correctly uses terms such as *before, after,* or *later* in his conversation.

It does not seem to bother children that time on television can pass very rapidly over several months or years. They rarely question or even consider that it is happening. They also fail to realize that television shows, such as westerns with Indians in them, or science fiction, do not represent present-day life. This became evident to me in my first grade class in a suburban school near Indianapolis. A musical group, comprised of native Americans from British Columbia, Canada, was visiting in the home of one of the teachers. One of the young men from the band offered to come over and talk to the children about his Indian heritage. As he walked by the school window approaching the building, one of the children said, "I think I saw an Indian, a real Indian." The man had long black hair and was wearing a simple head band so he resembled Indians the children had seen on television. As soon as the children settled down, he talked with them a while and then asked if they had any questions. The first question asked was, "How many white men have you scalped?" The children knew only the western stories they had seen on television and had no idea how present-day Indians live.

Time is probably most relevant to children's play in terms of how activities fit into their day. "Lunchtime," "naptime," "supper time," and "bedtime" all are a part of most children's daily routine until the age of three or four. "Time for school" may be added for nursery school, day care, or the babysitter. If parents work, there is the added "time for Mother (or Daddy) to pick you up." These time-appointed activities help the child develop some sense of time relationships. Added to that are "Saturday cartoons" and "church on Sunday" for some families, as well as "Mother or Daddy's day off from work." These additions contribute to the sense of week.

The child's sense of holidays advances with age, although relatively little spontaneous play occurs in the preschool years related to the major holidays. Some school activities focus attention on such things as the Pilgrims at Thanksgiving; elves, reindeer, Rudolph and Frosty at Christmas; and the Easter Bunny at Easter. These are usually more teacher-directed dramatizations than on the spot reenactments by the children.

Existence of Space

There are many theories and ideas regarding how children develop an understanding of the space surrounding them. Very early in infancy children attempt to orient themselves to their world. This is, of course, limited until they become more mobile and can crawl and walk. We have observed, however, that some sense of space is being formed by the way the baby is held during feeding. Some doctors recommend that the bottle-fed baby be alternated from the right arm to the left arm just as a breast-fed baby is held. Thus, both sides of the baby receive warmth and security from the parent.

Observations of infants indicate that they cannot retain concepts of where something is or how it is placed. The old adage, "out of sight, out of mind" seems to apply. Later, as toddlers, they can play simple "hide and seek" games. One thing that is noted in this stage is their inability to anticipate another location for a hidden object or person. They consistently look for the object or the person in the last place seen.

By the age of three, children have some ideas about how blocks and toys fill up space although they probably still try to ride their tricycles through spaces that are too small, or attempt to fit puzzle pieces into improbable spaces, or fit toy parts together inaccurately. Space concepts seem to be centered in the motor facility as demonstrated by the child's ability to stack a tower of blocks, gather a set of nesting toys.

The three-year-old child has a sense of *under, on,* and *in* and will use these terms in play. A little later the child's use of *where* indicates the acquisition of some sense of permanent location. When playing with toys such as a doll house or garage, the furniture or cars are placed so that some understanding of space, for example, in relation to the rooms in which certain furniture is placed, is shown.

At the next stage of development, we find the child using and apparently understanding the concepts of *up* and *down.* This may mean that the space concept is so flexible that location and movements within space can be imagined. This suggests an internalized map of locations and space exists, constructed in part by associations between familiar objects and their customary location.

Jamey's behavior provides an illustration of this developing, internalized mapping process. As a four year old, he was driven daily to a nursery school. One day, while his parents were painting, some old newspapers were lying on the floor. He discovered one that contained a full-size map of the town in which he lived. He became very excited about it and wanted to know where his house was located on the map. The location was pointed out and he commented that the neighborhood elementary school must be the large square just across his street. His mother pointed to the street which represented the one in front of their house and asked him if he could tell how to get to his nursery school. Since his street went directly to the shopping center, which was adjacent to the church in which his nursery school was held, he was able to follow the street to the shopping center and determine which way to turn to get to the church. Thus, it seems that some four year olds can internalize maps of familiar areas.

By late preschool and kindergarten, children acquire some understanding of volume. They talk about cans, boxes, and buckets being full or empty.

Some will even use the term *half-full*. Much of this volume-related activity centers around sand, mud, and water where they fill and refill available containers. Although independent action with these substances is very important for children to internalize their concepts of volume, it is helpful to tell them how to describe what they are doing and how to define what they have. Comments using terms such as *full, empty,* or *half-full* are helpful.

The child's relative sense of distance also shows in his play. In the dress corner at nursery school, you may hear a child tell another to go, "all the way into the bathroom," to go to the store, "because the store is far away." Children talk about sitting "close to each other," or "far apart" at story time. Conversations about going to visit relatives are sprinkled with comments concerning the time it takes to get there and how far away it is. Also, you may notice their attention to and increase in the language of location such as *by, between,* and *in front of.*

By school age, children have or are developing the concept of left-right as it applies to them. Their use of left-right concepts is not spontaneous, but may be included in activities to which children can respond. The left-right concept as it pertains to other things develops somewhat later and is still relative to the sides of their own bodies.

Now the child uses many spatial-concept words in play. Putting trains *through* tunnels, blocks on *top* of each other, a doll *inside* the dollhouse, the little bear in the *middle,* the father bear *next to* the little bear, and the belt *around* the doll are common phrases to primary age children. Other words such as *over, between, nearest, corner, row, center, side, below, forward, above, in order, behind, separated* are also prevalent.

One area of play where the developing concept of space can be observed is with blocks. At first, the child builds either by stacking a few blocks, or by laying them flat on the floor to develop roads, or to outline a structure. Gradually these structures take on form. The child begins to enclose the space by building walls with doors and windows. The use of special blocks allows for tunnels or structures resembling churches with steeples. By the primary years, the child can draw a model of the structure. This gives some indication of perception of dimensions of height and width.

Judgments are made on the basis of visual perception rather than on constancy of an area well into the early childhood years. The child believes what is seen rather than what really may be, which often leads to frustration and tears when a misjudgment is made. However, we recognize that it is probably impossible to tell a child what constancy of an area is, and that it is a developmental concept that must be acquired. Problems may develop though, if a child thinks someone else has more space or more toys when in reality the difference is in size. For example, two children are given equal space on a table to play. If one child chooses toys which take up a lot of space, this child may believe the other child has more room. Or in another situation, two children may be playing with an equal number of toys. The child with the smaller toys may feel the other child has more toys to play with.

Topographic and Weather Phenomena

Left to their own devices, children find many things in nature to play with. They use rocks, sticks, logs, water, seeds, and many other materials to make tools and devise games. Children love to climb on large rocks. They pretend they are ships, airplanes, space ships, and other machines. They make up jumping-off games and see who can scramble up the fastest or jump the farthest. They love water and unless given a reason to fear it they will attempt to play in it even when it is unsafe. Splashing and playing around in water is considered great fun. The combination of playing with sand and water on the beach is very enjoyable even for very young children. Young children who have no fear of water must be watched carefully since they do not realize the dangers inherent in playing in lakes, rivers, and pools.

Children love to explore the outdoors. Hiding under bushes, climbing hills and trees, and walking through woods gives them great opportunities for discovering how our world is put together. It also provides a wonderful opportunity for dramatizing television programs they have seen, like *Daniel Boone* or *Little House on the Prairie*.

Rain and snow hold a special fascination for children. They love to play in the snow—pull on a sled, roll around, or toss snowballs in the air. They also like to play in a warm rain, especially if puddles form that they can splash in. Although care should be taken to protect children from the cold, they should be encouraged to play in the snow, and when conditions are right, in the rain.

How Things Work

Young children have a lot of curiosity which seems to grow with them. From the time they try to put lids on bottles and boxes, fit blocks into the right slots of a toy, or take apart a telephone or a radio, children seek to find out how things work. New toys often end up in pieces because the child wants to see what makes the noise inside or how the handle works. They are interested in pulleys and in equipment that they can take apart, such as telephones and radios. Chemistry experiments intrigue children. They are fascinated with how vinegar and soda can pop the cork off a bottle, or with their discovery that the snowball they put in the bathtub disappeared. Interest in experimenting emerges rather early—in some cases, as early as four and five years old when parents or teachers make many such opportunities to experiment available.

Throughout the early childhood years, children incorporate into their play the things they are learning about. This chapter reviewed how children understand and master the physical environment. Much of what they come into contact with leads them to develop concepts and lays the foundation for later higher level thinking.

NOTES

1. Burton L. White, *The First Three Years of Life* (Englewood Cliffs, New Jersey: Prentice-Hall, 1975).

2. Suzuki developed a method whereby young children learn to play the violin by ear. Parents practice with the children at home. The Orff-Kodaly method involves the mastery of certain musical skills, like hearing, recognizing, and singing prescribed melodic intervals, and recognizing and playing prescribed rhythms before playing a specific instrument is taught. The development of musical concepts is carefully planned and sequenced.

CHAPTER
FOUR

*In sociodramatic play, children can display their physical
and creative abilities and their social awareness.*

Understanding and Mastering the Social Environment

During their early years, children spend much time and effort learning about their social environment. They must establish relationships with family members and with others outside the family. To establish relationships, they must learn how to interact with parents, other adults, and other children, and they must develop behavioral controls and social skills that make them acceptable in their family, neighborhood, and school. In addition, they must learn about family and occupational roles and become aware of the realities of the social world. Achieving these skills, that is, living with others in social situations, is dependent in part on their ability to communicate, verbally and nonverbally, and their ability to understand emotional expressions. In this chapter, we will show how play helps children understand their social environment. We will show also how play contributes to communication, to interacting with others, to mastering social skills, and to learning behavioral controls. In relation to each of these, we will describe how individual behavior develops and how play can be guided to contribute to this development.

In Chapter One, we referred to the literature published in the 1960s which placed as little emphasis on play as the earlier studies. During the 1960s, as a result of their concern for providing the best academic education for young children, many educators forgot to consider the interrelatedness of all aspects of development. They concentrated on academic development and neglected development in the affective area. Understanding the social environment is an important accomplishment. If, however, educators do not feel that this is a sufficient reason for including play in planning children's learning programs, they should consider the fact that development in affective areas can influence children's development in cognitive areas, which is an equally important reason for helping children master the social environment.

In Chapter Two we described *reproductive play,* which occurs between the ages of four and seven, as children are reproducing social realities. They imagine themselves in different social roles in which they imitate what adults do and say in like situations. We defined *dramatic play* as the child playing alone, sometimes using trucks, blocks, or dolls to reproduce social situations. We defined *play* as sociodramatic when more than one child is involved in reproductive play. In this chapter we will use the terms *dramatic* and *socio-dramatic play* rather than the more inclusive term *reproductive play.* This chapter will show that sociodramatic play—as opposed to dramatic play—is the more mature means of understanding the social environment. We have also included research which supports the importance of sociodramatic play, and we have included some of the ways of stimulating and guiding socio-dramatic play.

Role of Dramatic and Sociodramatic Play

One important aspect of both dramatic play and sociodramatic play is imitation. Children do what they see adults do. They try to act, talk, and dress to look like people they know. In their imitative action and speech, children are sometimes surprisingly accurate in reproducing what they have seen others do. They play fire fighters by driving the truck, ringing the bell, and wearing a red hat. They pretend to shout directions to other firefighters as they busily put out fires with old pieces of hose removed from make believe fire trucks. Obviously, there is also an imaginative element in play. Through make believe children can overcome the limitations of reality in time and space and make possible a richer reproduction of real life events. In such play, communication (usually verbal) is necessary, because without it, other children will not understand the make believe elements and cannot respond to them.

Sociodramatic play includes imitation, imagination or make believe, and interaction with other children. Smilansky[1] lists six criteria that are helpful in observing and evaluating sociodramatic play. These criteria are

(a) imitative role play
(b) make believe in regard to objects

(c) make believe in regard to actions and situations
(d) persistence
(e) interaction
(f) verbal communication

The complexity of children's behavior increases as they reach the different levels. The first four criteria generally apply to dramatic play; the last two apply to sociodramatic play only.

In dramatic play, the child imitates another person's action and speech with the aid of real or imagined objects. Often movements or verbal declarations are substituted for real objects. The child's verbalization is imitative and may also be substituted for actions and situations. Verbalization may also have a make believe element as the child uses it to change identity ("I am the firefighter to put out the fires"), to change the identity of objects (An acorn from the playground becomes food on a plate) and to substitute speech for action ("Let's pretend we have already eaten breakfast, and you are the daddy who is going to work") though in reality the children have been playing separately and may continue to do so. Dramatic play also requires a continuation of the role for a reasonable period of time as opposed to momentary, pretend play.

Sociodramatic play includes all of the elements previously listed, but in addition, there must be interaction between at least two players and some verbal interaction (which does not necessarily accompany dramatic play). Sociodramatic play does not always include all of these elements, but there must be some imitative behavior, some make believe, and some kind of play-related interaction.

There is no clear age distinction between the ages at which children begin dramatic and sociodramatic play. Direct imitation of adults, such as feeding a doll, occurs at the beginning of the second year; but sociodramatic play requires verbalization and, therefore, does not usually begin until about the third year. At about three years of age, children begin to seek the company of other children, and from then until about six years of age, children frequently engage in sociodramatic play. Beginning at age seven, sociodramatic play tends to decrease and games with rules become more common in the child's play behavior. Socioeconomic differences and differences in emotional and intellectual development result in some variation in the play of individual children.

The importance of sociodramatic play lies in the opportunity that it provides for children to display their physical accomplishments, creative abilities, and their social awareness in ways that can be satisfying in developing relationships with the adult world. Children can react on the basis of their knowledge of the adult world and experiences of the objective world, but they satisfy their personal needs and wishes through imagination. They can assume roles that are not, in reality, available to children. They can be successful at feats for which their skills are not yet adequate and can satisfy wishes which cannot be met in the real world.

Evidence is beginning to accumulate that all children do not necessarily engage in sociodramatic play. It appears that only a minimal sort of play can be taken for granted. Participation skills in highly elaborate sociodramatic play are apparently learned. One dramatic example of children's need to be taught to play was mentioned in Chapter One. Pavenstedt [2] found that pre-school children from disorganized lower class families did not know how to play. The children in this study often used their bodies for diffuse discharge of energy and avoidance of involvement and were unable to focus on the pleasures of attaining mastery. These children acted upon clues, or in indirect imitation of others, rather than by developing activities of their own volition. In nursery school, transitions were the most difficult part of the school routine, because these children could not focus on the job to be done. They showed a striking unresponsiveness to large segments of their external world, yet heightened auditory, and particularly, visual alertness with excessive focusing on adult actions. They showed little knowledge or curiosity about their environment, and expectations of calamity and guarded fearfulness permeated all aspects of their coping mechanisms. These children did not know how to play. Their demarcation between reality and fantasy appeared unusually poor, and being in contact with adults took precedence over all else.

These children's progress in relating to the social environment was very slow. But after two years in nursery school, they showed a more trusting, warm, affectionate response to their teacher, and their peer relationships developed to a point of age-appropriate behavior. Almost all of the children observed could share and cooperate. They began to enjoy play and developed the capacity to become involved. There was a shift from diffuse, motoric tension discharge to a more focused mode of reacting to stress, which frequently included verbalizations.

In a very extensive study of children's sociodramatic play, Smilansky [3] reports that so-called "disadvantaged" children do not engage in sociodramatic play. Since this study involved both advantaged and disadvantaged children, Smilansky was able to provide a contrast in the behavior of children from these two socioeconomic backgrounds. The sociodramatic play of all the culturally advantaged children involved a variety of themes and roles centered around social problems of the adults with whom the children had the closest contact. These included home and family themes; professional roles, such as doctor, nurse, pilot, sailor, teacher; kindergarten and nursery school themes, such as birthday parties; and dramatizations, such as circus and zoo. The advantaged children's play did not differ in the themes chosen but rather in the diversity and variety of roles undertaken, in the range and depth of relationships portrayed, and in the degree to which the play process indicated an understanding of the main factors involved in a given social situation.

The disadvantaged children used toys mostly in manipulative ways, duplicating and reduplicating conventional motor activities. They used miniature replicas of objects in the adult world in much the same way as adults use them. Their use of toys was rigid and seemed to have great importance for them. The advantaged children seemed to prefer less well-defined play objects that could serve several purposes, and they could substitute verbal descriptions for toy-connected activity. For the most part, the games of disadvantaged children were played between the child and the play object. Manipulation of and involvement with the play object, rather than verbalization, provided the means for identification with the role being enacted. There was a difference in the verbalization of the two groups in quality and content but little difference in quantity. For example, the advantaged children used much more complex sentence structure and talked about a greater number of subjects, but the amount of speech for both groups was about the same.

Behavior of the leaders of the two groups differed widely. It was immediately apparent who was the leader of the disadvantaged children. The leader would start a game by asserting leadership, assume a role of authority, give orders, act to maintain authority, and use whatever means necessary to maintain power. In many advantaged groups, there appeared to be two leaders, and often it was difficult to spot the leader. In case of conflict, the leaders and the other participants tended to review the situation and resolve the conflict through discussion. The children appeared to be imitating the leadership roles they had seen enacted in their homes.

None of the existing literature on play explains the lack of sociodramatic play in large groups of children, so Smilansky engaged in an analysis of the child-rearing attitudes and practices of families. From interviews and observations in the homes of the children, essential differences in child-rearing attitudes and practices were apparent. Although homes of both advantaged and disadvantaged children seemed to provide the warm, emotional relationships necessary for children to identify with adults, the disadvantaged homes failed to equip the children with training and encouragement in the basic techniques of sociodramatic play. For children from these homes, the natural processes of child growth and the nondirective, enriched environment in the preschool and kindergarten were not enough to give them the necessary boost, unless there was a degree of positive intervention by parents and/or teachers. Smilansky also discovered that analytic therapy requiring conversation with the children was not effective with them. When she switched to play therapy, she quickly discovered that they did not know how to play imaginatively and could not be helped in that manner, either. Her studies also reveal that provision of cognitive experiences alone would not boost the disadvantaged children's play abilities; but if teachers play with the children, they can benefit from new knowledge and experiences. Teaching children how to play increased their level of imaginative activity—and with it, their persistence in play, their social interaction, and their capacity for verbal communication.

Also related to Smilansky's findings was the research of Hess et al.[4] in which they found that the family provides a hidden curriculum for the middle class child. Middle class mothers in this study were able to teach their children how to put simple puzzles together and play simple games. They could communicate the task to be accomplished and help the children acquire the needed skills. The lower class mothers wanted their children to learn, but were unable to communicate to the children what they needed to do in order to achieve success. Viewed from the perspective of the children's need for success in play activities, this research also supports the children's need to be taught to play.

Freyburg,[5] in a subsequent study of lower class kindergarten children, found that by playing with them she could increase their level of imaginative play. She found that at the beginning of her study the children were extremely unimaginative in their play. They introduced no pretend play elements into the play situation and were extremely stimulus-bound by the play materials, with no role taking and a very concrete use of the play materials. After the teachers played with the children, their play shifted to a higher level of originality in the ways they used toys and play materials, and they began to use a high amount of pretend elements in their play. Their play was a highly organized role-playing activity in which the children were able to go well beyond the play stimuli as well as to resist interruption by others.

Since children without some encouragement from adults can be expected to engage in play only minimally, as an early education teacher, you have the responsibility to help children develop the skills necessary for sociodramatic play. It is also possible that children in your classroom may differ widely in their need for assistance in learning to play. Without assistance, some children will become involved in learning academic skills without acquiring some of the adaptive abilities and self-discipline necessary for success. One of the properties of sociodramatic play is that it enables children to develop an adaptive capacity for varied behavior. Teaching children to play, then, is one way to help them avoid developing adaptive deficits.

Guiding Sociodramatic Play

First, we will talk about some general ways you can help children who do not engage in sociodramatic play. You must learn to take an active part in the children's environment, and model some of the behaviors you want them to learn. Prior to this you need to provide the opportunity for the children to play on their own, possibly engaging in the same activity repeatedly or jumping continuously from one activity to another until you see they are stuck. At this point, you can plan the appropriate intervention. You do not *talk* about the play, rather you begin to play by becoming one of the participants, such as a truck driver, a mother giving her baby a bottle, or a salesperson selling shoes. You become an active participant in the play by making suggestions, comments, demonstrating activities or using other means relevant to the situation. In this way, you can make the children aware of different play possibilities and of experiences and memories from which they can draw. They can act as they want without having to face all the problems of self-expression alone and unaided. You can provide the stimulus to make sociodramatic play a pleasant and satisfying experience.

A word of caution about how you enter into the play is necessary. You must continue to remain in the adult role as a facilitator rather than trying to force the child into a leadership role. You also must not act as another child. You clearly must remain in the leadership role in order to relinquish it at the appropriate time. You must also remember that you are responsible for all of the children in the class, and organize activities in a way that will enable you to leave without interrupting the play more than necessary.

Be careful about trying to stimulate play by directing questions to the children to actively engage them in play. Such questions, directed to children who do not already know how to play, are not helpful. Feitelson [6] found "What do you want to play?" was a fatal beginning for a teaching session. Interest and rapport are also stopped by such questions as "Here is a doll. What shall we name her?" or "Look at this nice bus. Where is it going?" An equally bad question at the conclusion of a play episode is "What shall we do now?" If the children have had no real experience with imaginative play, you cannot expect them to be able to provide initiative in such situations. If you go into the "kitchen" and pretend to prepare a meal, explaining your activity as you go along, "We will need to prepare something special for the doll, because she will not eat salad. We will prepare meat, potatoes, and other foods." The children may be able to add "milk" or "bread and butter" at this point. If there are two or more dolls in the housekeeping area, and you pick up a doll and pretend to feed it, making a munching sound, the children may pick up other dolls and imitate what you are doing.

The suggestions just described may seem strange to you if you have been teaching middle class children in nursery school or kindergarten and were successful without entering into their activities. You may even have been taught not to engage in play with children. If so, analyze the situation. Do the children need your help? Do they have ideas of their own? Do they start to play on their own or must they have help? Not all children need the intervention previously described and children who do not need it may be inclined to resent such intervention. Clearly, you must adjust your intervention to the children's needs and to their previous experiences.

Children who have not mastered the sensorimotor and constructive phases of the uses of various materials—how to use the materials, what the materials will do—will not be able to use these materials as props for understanding the social environment. Your responsibility as a teacher may be to provide more exploratory experiences prior to engaging a child in sociodramatic play. You must also examine their relationships with other people. Children, generally, must establish some kind of meaningful relationships with adults before they are able to participate in socialized play with other children. It is unlikely that a child will move into sociodramatic play until a comfortable relationship has been established with adults. You may initiate an activity, such as a cooking experience, in which the children have positive experiences with you as the adult leader and have positive interactions with the other children. They can enjoy the project together and share in the best result of all, the eating. Such experiences help to build respect for and trust in you as a person and help to establish the basis from which you can become a successful teacher in actual play situations.

Almost all children will have had some experiences that can become the basis for sociodramatic play, such as observing the activities of their mother feeding the baby, cutting grass, driving a car, or cleaning house. They can model their father's activities as he washes dishes, digs the garden, plays a guitar, or polishes shoes. There is a range of behaviors mothers and fathers or other caregivers model for their children. However, the fact that children have had certain experiences does not mean that they can use them in play. Enlarging a child's environment at the same time that he is being taught to play seems to help in the use of experiences. Understanding the social environment requires that a child have varied experience with it.

If we compare the experiences of low income, rural children, six to eight years old, with the experiences of the well-traveled, middle income children of the same age, it is apparent that the middle class children have a distinct advantage. Children who travel see things that do not appear in their home environment. They stay in motels, eat in restaurants and experience different climates. They have more varied recreation experiences. Some middle income children learn various physical skills, such as swimming and team games, and they attend children's theater and may take dancing or music lessons. Even the houses in which they live and the activities pursued by different members of their families provide a background that is helpful in creating their play activities. Some parents do a remarkably good job enriching their child's background. Yet, you can nearly always enlarge upon children's abilities to observe. Even with all their experiences, children often have gaps in what they have experienced in their immediate neighborhoods. Their parents sometimes overlook something. Some things are especially difficult for parents to arrange. Whether the experiences with the social environment have been very broad or very limited, you can usually enlarge upon them. Even parents who do not take their children places will often go with you if you make the arrangements. You may wish to do two things: (a) arrange some excursions as part of the school curriculum, and (b) suggest some places for parents to take their children which will be easy for the family, but which would not be appropriate to arrange for a class. A list of some possible excursions is included in Appendix B.

Part of the task of enlarging upon children's social environment is your sensitivity to their interests. A three-year-old child visiting the zoo for the first time does not need to be shown the whole zoo. If there is a children's zoo, a three year old could just be taken there, or in a large zoo just go to see the large animals. It depends in part on the size of the zoo and how long it takes to see it. Children this age will need to be given the names of the animals and helped to observe some specific characteristics of each animal, such as its eyes, neck, fur, and the sounds it makes. This creates an ideal situation for communication between adults and children as you talk about what they have seen and are excited about.

Sociodramatic Play and Communication Skills

Communication is essential to the development and progression of a socio-dramatic play episode. The child's language development, therefore, becomes an important consideration in sociodramatic play. Younger preschool children repeat words or sounds in imitation of adults, but much of their communication includes gestures, grunts, and tugging at the adult to substitute for lack of language proficiency. Usually, by the time they enter nursery school, children comprehend sentences in context quite well, but still do not have the language facility to mediate in social situations. In addition, language is quite egocentric. After about four years of age, the child uses compound and complex sentences, expresses ideas based on experience, shares information and impressions, and can tell a complete version of something that has happened. In addition, the child can use language imaginatively in storytelling and in play. Typically, in kindergarten and primary school, some aspects of language develop rapidly. If you consider all of early childhood, you can see that play contributes to the child's ability to explain, describe, articulate, express feelings, comprehend statements and questions, use typical sentence constructions, seek information, and use nonverbal cues. (See Chapter Two.)

Children must talk to let other children know what they are thinking and doing. Language in play is an imitation of adult speech used for conveying imaginative and make believe themes, and to manage the play in the form of discussion, commands, directions, and explanations. Sometimes words take the place of actions which the children cannot or choose not to perform. Each participant in sociodramatic play takes cues from the lines spoken by other participants and supplies verbal cues in turn. Smilansky [7] points out the most essential difference in the verbalization of advantaged and disadvantaged children is a difference in quality and content, rather than in quantity. Advantaged children kept up a constant chatter relevant to the role being enacted. They used words acquired from others to express concepts and to feed their ideas back to the other children. Disadvantaged children, who were engaged more in the manipulation of objects, used verbal expression to manage the game being played. This game was largely a physical action between a child and a play object. The role and theme-related speech enriches play and adds a source of satisfaction not available in action-oriented play. This enrichment occurs through the additional self-expression and reward that children receive when they express in words the things that they visualize in imagination. Verbal expression also helps to keep the play situation moving the way the children want it to, and the experience of hearing themselves talk aloud helps to blend their speech and action with the speech and action of others. They also get satisfaction from increasing their word power.

What you do to facilitate verbal communication depends a great deal upon the levels at which children are functioning. You may put into words what children seem to need to communicate but do not know how. You may provide an elaboration of what children have said, although such direct intervention may not be acceptable. Children who engage in a high level of sociodramatic play usually do not want you to participate directly in their activities. If you do this, it only disrupts their play. Your role is the more indirect one of ensuring that there is a steady input in information, vocabulary, and concepts on the themes that the children select. Your input provides stimulation to try out new learning or to adapt concepts into their already existing conceptual framework. Since verbal communication constantly accompanies play, the alert teacher observes carefully and listens intently without being obtrusive and acts at the appropriate time to fill in the gaps in the children's knowledge and vocabulary. If needed, the teacher supplies props which children are unable to invent from their existing store of blocks, toys, and art supplies.

If a child's verbalization serves only to link the activity to the objects being played with, the task is quite different. Verbal communication should change from focusing on objects to focusing on other children. Children must become involved with each other for this level of language to develop. There are two things you can do simultaneously that are reinforcing. The first is to provide teacher-directed activities, as previously mentioned, such as a cooking experience that you lead, but requiring the children to cooperate in a group to produce a satisfying result. For example, you could provide a tray with water and some objects that will float and some that will not. Children will usually gather around the activity and want to participate. You can make it easier still by providing two pans of water. The idea is essentially that the children are participating together in a similar activity. Their language, in part, is directed to the other children because there are usually some conflicts, but there are also shared satisfactions. The children usually cannot participate without being brought into contact with other children, but they do not have to assume full responsibility for maintaining order because you will be there to handle whatever is beyond them and to provide clues for their behavior: "Sammy, you have room on this side, please move over so Sue will have room for her objects." "Tell Mario he may not have the boat until you have finished using it."

The second thing you can do is to play with the children using toys and materials, such as blocks and housekeeping materials that are in the room to be used freely by the children for sociodramatic play. Sit down in the block area and start to stack or build a very simple structure with the blocks. As you do this, hand a supply of blocks to children who will almost certainly gather around you. Talk to them about what you are building and invite them to become a part of the building project. Use language to engage the children in the play as you build. "If we had some animals, this could be the barn." "We could park the car in the garage, while we build a road to the city." At first, you supply the language to provide both the imaginative and verbal aspects of the play. You can guide the interaction so that the children's lack of skill does not continuously end in destructive behavior, and so that the group stays a manageable size. The children are not actually engaged in sociodramatic play, but they are acquiring some of the skills that will facilitate their engagement in the play. They are using verbal communication to understand and manage the behavior of other children.

Two other steps will often be necessary: intervention from inside the play and intervention from outside. Intervention from the inside is an extension of the previously described block-building episode. You choose a role and enact it for a period of time. You may be the doctor who has come to see the sick baby. Pretending to hand the mother the medicine, you may say, "Here is the medicine that will make your baby better. Be sure to give it to her every two hours." "You will need to call a nurse, because your baby is very sick and needs special care." You then respond to the cues that the children accept, extending the play to keep various children involved.

Intervention may also take the form of your staying outside the role, especially if the children already engage in some kind of role taking. You must follow the play closely so that you understand the roles that the children take. Suggestions should be made in terms of the roles assumed by the children. You address the role person with suggestions ("Let's see which pair of shoes will fit this customer"), questions ("Where will your truck deliver groceries today?"), directions ("Show the nurse where the telephone is so she can telephone the doctor"), or clarification of behavior ("He wants a place to park his truck, too"). Sometimes, acting outside the role, yet in terms of it, you can help to establish contact when players are unable to do it themselves. ("Someone is knocking on your door. It is your neighbor bringing a present for your baby's birthday.") Only practice and accurate assessment of the children's readiness will enable you to be successful with these techniques. Remember that your purpose is to promote a response, not to control the play. And remember, a child will not respond to every attempted intervention. Children should also be given only the assistance they need. A little success may cause you to intervene more than is necessary or desirable, so be cautious and sensitive to the children's readiness and need to be helped. The level of verbal communication will be greatest when children are finally able to sustain their own activity in sociodramatic play.

You may encourage communication in nonverbal as well as verbal ways. For example, you may sit on a block and pretend that you are driving a car, or you may go into the kitchen and pretend to mix a cake. Your acting gives the child the idea that it is acceptable to pretend. If you are invited to share lunch with the pretend family, you can pretend to eat and comment on how good the food is, using a combination of verbal and nonverbal communication.

Nonverbal behavior to facilitate communication does not always require direct intervention into children's play. A more indirect approach that many teachers use to facilitate communication in nonverbal ways is to structure a new play setting or restructure a setting that seems to be causing problems. You may not say a word, but when you see that there are too many children in the housekeeping area you may set up a table (plainly visible) outside the area to wash the dishes used. This creates a second play area, introduces a new idea into the play, and provides new roles for some of the children.

Once the crowding is reduced, it is easier for the children to communicate and fewer conflicts result.

It may seem that this section has said more about techniques to guide play than about facilitating communication. Do not be misled. Communication skills of children are most evident in situations in which the children have a real need to convey an idea, and the situation in which this can most naturally occur is in sociodramatic play. In sociodramatic play there is a strong motivational factor in both a social and intellectual sense. Children can be very proud of the roles they assume because they are impressed by what they have seen adults do. Play also provides a means to try out their impressions and receive a reaction with a minimum threat of failure. This setting is more natural and spontaneous than adult-directed group settings requiring conformity and possible correction.

Interaction with Others

Young preschool children are emotionally attached to a small group of adults, including their immediate families, and they are dependent on them for many things. Young preschoolers need to have their mothers or a reasonable substitute nearby. Their social relationships are dependent and exploitive. When two children are together, they play parallel, largely ignoring each other. No preferences are shown for particular children. Development shows a rather typical pattern at the beginning of social play, with the child showing preference for one particular companion. At this point in socialization, the child still wants things his own way, and social relationships tend to be filled with a conflict of wills. Gradually relationships become more reciprocal; there is a greater amount of give and take, and loyalty to particular people develops. The child develops a preference for particular friends and verbally expresses these preferences. Social relationships deepen. By the age of eight, the child gives much greater attention and interest to other children and is much less in need of other people's help and protection. Play is one of the major processes through which this adjustment takes place. Adults at home and in school are frequently involved. The earliest play experiences occur at home, but by the time many children are interested in other children, they are enrolled in nursery school.

Friendly interactions with their parents greatly facilitate friendly interactions with strangers, either children or adults. During the second and third year, parents must be willing to meet their children's demands for attention and dependency, and at the same time, allow them to explore activities with other children. In these early developmental stages parents do many things indirectly which facilitate the interactions between their children and other children. One thing parents can do is to plan for their children to have positive interactions with other adults. Adults, other than parents, can be included in family activities and can be encouraged to play with very young children in a familiar setting, with familiar adults nearby, so that there is no threat to security. Mothers with other young children who are family friends may visit in each other's homes, taking their children along. Once children are familiar with the other children and adults, they could visit without their parents.

In infancy, children should be played with in ways that enable them to feel satisfaction from both the play and the personal contact. As children begin to show interest in toys, you can demonstrate what the toys will do and give the child a chance to imitate. Build with ABC blocks to show that they can be stacked, and provide the opportunity for children to knock them down long before there is any interest in stacking them up. In this way, children have the opportunity to see what can be done with their toys and can interact in a fun way. Eventually, they will imitate the building and expect friendly interactions with those who play with them.

If you have been around young children very much, you know that an adult's presence makes the play more satisfying, and the variety of uses for materials that adults introduce exceeds the child's uses for them. As children play and adults laugh and play with them, the play activity is reinforced. When children become interested in parallel play, this same kind of interaction can be continued. Most of the interaction will be between you and a child rather than among the children.

A very important step in three to six-year-old children's interactions with others is their entry into school—nursery school, kindergarten, or even primary grades if they have had no previous experience in groups—because this necessitates interactions with strange adults and with children. This step can be eased considerably by the parent who plans ahead for the first day of school, or the teacher who plans a transition period for new children. If you are planning the school opening day, there are several steps you may take to assist children's adjustment. You can hold a meeting in the spring for parents who expect to enroll children for the fall session, at which time information can be given to help them prepare their children for school entry. You can suggest such simple procedures as inviting a child who may be in the group next year to visit for a short time, first with the mother present and then without her. You can suggest to parents that they provide an opportunity for children to spend the afternoon with their grandmother or with a friend, first at home and later at grandmother's or the friend's home, to help them relate to other adults. Gradually increasing the territory around the home in which children are comfortable helps them to feel more independent although still under supervision. Talk about school in a pleasant way but do not "oversell" as school may have a hard time living up to the super buildup. If at all possible, you should invite children who will be going to school the next year to come for a visit. In the spring, when nursery school and kindergarten children typically are proud of their independence, they are willing to invite a younger child into their play for a short time. Be sure the visit occurs when there is free activity enabling exploration of some of the materials in the room. You probably know some parents who will do these things anyway, but some others will need to be reminded that a certain degree of independence helps children feel more comfortable during their first days of school.

There are other ways you can ease these first days of school, if you have the support of your administrator. The first days of school should be kept simple and short. It is much better for children not to want to go home than to cry because mother has not come. The younger the children the more essential short, simple days are, especially for three year olds just starting nursery school. Another thing you may do is invite parents and children to come for an open house or a visit the week before school begins. The parent may show the child around then stay in the background to give the child a chance to explore with other children and to give you a chance to initiate some contact. On this day, it may be very important that the parent initiate no comments about leaving. In addition to helping the child become familiar with the classroom, this visit helps you develop some hypotheses about the ease with which the child will adjust to school. Those children who are able to leave their parent and play with other children and who are able to relate to you seldom have serious adjustment difficulties. Those who stand beside their parent and do not relate to you or the other children may need to do considerably more watching with the parent present before interacting comfortably with anyone else. If no one pushes these children to take steps they are not ready for, they will gradually venture toward an interesting toy or possibly sit with other children for a glass of juice. Efforts to entice such children into activity need to be quite subtle as they tend to withdraw from direct approaches.

Other steps you may take include shortening the time children stay in school for the first day or two, possibly three or four days for a few children, and keeping the number of children small during the first few days. If the program is an all-day program, keep the first days short enough to delay naps until children have been in school long enough to feel comfortable with the adults. Children who seem ready for school can soon begin a regular schedule and special arrangements can be made for children who need additional precautions. A gradual transition will enable most children to interact comfortably with both adults and children.

Children's desires to interact with other children do not mean that they have the skills to play cooperatively. Relationships are often quite stormy when three and four-year-old children first begin to play together. They want to play together, but their relationships are alternately cooperative and quarrelsome. They begin to have special friends that they play with but they still want their own way. So their play tends to be a mixture of affection and selfishness, friendship and competition. They can be sociable until the desire for the same toy or the first turn results in a conflict of wills. Fortunately, language abilities are also developing rapidly which helps them to learn ways of coping with other children's wants.

At this level of interaction, your techniques of working with children are very important. Consistent patience and firmness are required. Since children imitate adult behavior, modeling both the language and the actions you want them to use provides a guide for their use in future situations. Firmness is required in the sense that adults should be consistent in communicating what is expected.

At this point, we need to refer to some of the ideas discussed in the general techniques for guiding sociodramatic play and in the use of play to facilitate communication skills. The focus here is a little different since the goal is not to stimulate play but to guide the interactions. Still, sociodramatic play provides the interaction which children must learn to cope with. They are free to choose whom and what they will play with and these choices often lead to conflicts.

Children must have both the desire to interact positively with others and some skill in doing so. In the play situation, you can patiently explain behavior that you plan to support: "Jim had the truck first; you may have it when he has finished. I will help you find a car to use while you wait." "Susan is first; Jeff is second; Martin is third. . . ." "When you go down the slide, move away from the bottom so the next person can come down safely." "Tell Ali it hurts when he hits." "Ask Rita if you may have a turn when she has finished." "I do not know who had that piece of clay first, but here is another piece so you both may have some."

Not all of the techniques you need to help children interact with one another are verbal. Some demand only action. When children seem to be close to conflict, you can simply move closer to them. Your presence may be enough of a reminder that you will enforce previous action and the potential offender (who probably knows he is the offender) may stop the unacceptable behavior. Sometimes you can prevent a block building from undergoing sure destruction by placing yourself between the building and the possible offender. It is also supportive if you can maintain direct eye contact with a child or when you gently place a hand on a shoulder. You can often be more successful in obtaining cooperation for such tasks as cleaning up after play if you simply start to put away blocks and other materials as you start to remind the children to do it. In some situations, the action serves to reinforce simultaneous speech. Possibly, many of the action techniques are effective because they reinforce what has already been communicated verbally.

Mastering Social Skills

Many adults think of social skills as the surface behaviors that children are taught so that they are socially acceptable to adults. Here we refer to the ability to say "please" and "thank you" at the appropriate time, not to interrupt adults, and to ask to be excused from the dinner table. These are important social behaviors because most families regard them so. If the parents or other significant adults are "polite" to each other and to the children, the children, with a little urging soon learn to "say" the right thing. We do not wish to underrate this kind of learning; however, there are more basic and significant social skills that we should be concerned with. These include recognizing and being able to label emotions, learning how someone feels by observing his facial expression, tone of voice, and listening to what he says, learning about realities of the social world, and becoming aware of family and other occupational roles. Some of these are often neglected in both home and school situations.

Learning social skills begins with the child's own experience and behavioral expression of emotion. Social skill imitation begins as sensorimotor imitation. Progress through the preschool years depends greatly upon the child's social-emotional relationship with his parents and the particular behavior that these models demonstrate for him. The child also tends to imitate those things he has seen rewarded or attended to by adults with another child. From nonverbal recognition of emotion, the child first begins to recognize "happy" and "mad." Later, if an adult has used a particular label for an emotion, the child uses it. The older kindergarten and beginning primary child can recognize age differences on the basis of facial cues. He knows the common family roles and imitates them in play. He is learning about roles outside his family in the world of work. From a low interest in other children and the inability to share, he becomes able to express appreciation of gratitude, show kindnesses toward those he likes, and express sympathy and concern. In dramatic play, he rehearses many positive social behaviors which he cannot yet use in real life situations.

Since children learn about adult roles through imitating the actions of adults, you should provide many opportunities for imitating adult roles in your classroom. Throughout this chapter much emphasis has been placed on dramatic play, and here again, sociodramatic play assumes a very important role. A classroom that provides props, such as hats for various occupations and dress-up clothes (e.g. work shirts, men's and women's shoes, neckties, aprons, uniforms, etc.) will encourage children to enact the adult behaviors they associate with the clothes. These props along with large blocks to construct busses, airplanes, ships, and trains that children can ride on, grocery stores, post offices, and filling stations where they can be the clerks or attendants, encourage children to imitate roles they observe in their neighborhoods or on television. You can be most successful if you acquaint yourself with the occupations that are most familiar to children in the neighborhood of your school and provide the props for those. This role play may also be facilitated by trips to local shops and industries, accompanied by explanations of what the workers do. Sometimes, the children are permitted to handle the equipment used by the workers. Books and films can be used to supplement the teaching of concepts which the children are unable to acquire from their own observation. Their understanding of different roles will increase greatly as they are encouraged to use new ideas and new props in their play.

Social skills can be enhanced or deterred depending upon the behavior of the adults who interact with children. This presents an unusually difficult problem for the teacher when it is known that the social skills that are being developed in the home are inadequate for the children's interactions outside the home. Earlier in this chapter, we referred to the difference in leadership style of the children from advantaged and disadvantaged backgrounds (Smilansky[8]). The advantaged children imitated the more democratic behavior of their parents, and the disadvantaged children imitated the more authoritarian leader pattern observed in their homes. The more democratic leadership pattern used verbal discussion to settle arguments, whereas the authoritarian leader used language to command. Furthermore, the advantaged children had a more generalized conception of roles enacted and were more willing to accept the role play of their peers. Disadvantaged children conceived roles in terms of observed activities and were not able to accept any behavior that deviated from these activity patterns. With this in mind, it becomes essential to demonstrate behaviors in the classroom which will help children become more sensitive to other people's feelings, teach them how to share, to have patience, and to cooperate in group endeavors.

Sociodramatic play and imitation are the means by which children learn the social skills which are not taught at home. Using the language and action you hope the children will imitate, and explaining reasons for your behavior makes your guidance an important tool. In order to use sociodramatic play for learning social skills, children must be taught to engage in it at levels that require both interaction and verbal communication. In order to learn how people respond to them and how to respond to other people, they must use play as a means of assuming a variety of roles and solving a variety of problems. These problems, whether they arise in the planning stage of the play, from the differing needs and behavior of the participants, from procuring the toys and props needed, or from the limited space available, offer the possibility of a variety of solutions which you can help the children consider. As they learn to consider alternatives, they become more flexible and their play can continue without interruption.

Also, children learn to recognize feelings through play. As they assume different roles and solve different problems, they experience many different emotions. At first, they experience the emotions nonverbally, but if you begin to put labels to these emotional experiences, they will gradually do the same. Some of the emotions are real, some are assumed. It is very real when a child is rejected by others and comes crying to you both for comfort and assistance. You may say "It really makes you sad when the other children won't let you play." Depending on the situation you may try to find a way to get the child into the play, or you may find another group more willing to add another playmate. A more usual response is to try to get admission to the group, but sometimes the circumstances demand a different response. Some children are rejected because of destructive or noncooperative behavior, and if the other children verbalize their reason for rejection, the child knows what must be done to get into the group. Sometimes it is tough for a child to face the consequences of his behavior, but this also is very important social learning.

All emotions expressed in play need not be negative ones. When children are very satisfied with their abilities, you can say "You feel very good that you can stack the blocks so high." or "Your block building will make a good garage for your car; that should make you very happy." This recognition of their real feelings and the ways that they show them will precede their ability to perceive emotions in role playing, although it may not precede their ability to show such emotions. In role playing you may use the same procedures. If children are playing "going to the beach," you could say "You have a happy face because you are going to the beach today," or "You enjoy playing in the water." In the housekeeping area, you could say "Your baby looks very scared, you need to hold him while he gets his shot." This kind of labeling helps in the recognition of an emotion.

Helping children recognize and express emotion may be difficult for you because of your own background. In our society, we do not always learn how to cope with our emotions. For example, if a child falls down and gets a skinned knee, some adults say "Don't cry, it doesn't hurt," instead of "It hurts, but we will clean it off and doctor it, so it won't hurt long." Some adults force children to say "I'm sorry" when they are everything except sorry; in fact they may be very angry and upset. It's much better to recognize how angry they are: "I know you're mad because they won't let you play, but I can't let you knock down their barn." This may help them gain control of their feelings. Adults who are uncomfortable with children's unpleasant feelings mean well, but they teach children to deny feelings rather than to learn to control them. It is amazing how hurt and anger can be decreased when someone understands the feeling and accepts it.

The child's ability to engage in certain positive social behaviors, such as showing kindness to those whom he likes and expressing empathy with a child who has been hurt or disappointed, is dependent upon his ability to see things from the perspective of others and ordinarily occurs toward the end of the early childhood years. Adults who have been empathetic with children, who have established good relationships with them, and who have established good relationships between siblings or children in a classroom, usually have modeled the behaviors they want children to imitate. Sociodramatic play also provides for rehearsal of behaviors, such as giving, inviting, and cooperating, which help the child to become socially acceptable.

Development of Behavioral Controls

The development of behavioral controls is usually a matter of overall maturity, so it is of great importance to understand what the child can comprehend. When they first enter nursery school, many children do not yet know what is good or bad behavior. They may even have been sent to nursery school because their newly discovered motor abilities enable them to get into everything resulting in conflicts with parents. Yet these children are too young to understand explanations. They respond to redirection, but they have no understanding of rules, and their responses to outside controls are lacking or weak.

Older preschool children understand "bad," but they do not fully understand "good." They will conform to what the adult requests if the adult is there to enforce the request. They obey rules for external reasons, such as to avoid punishment or disapproval, rather than for internal reasons, such as a belief that the rules are right. Gradually, rules come to have great importance. Primary children accept rules that have been set by adults but they cannot yet make true moral judgments on the basis of fact. In the process of learning behavioral controls, children must give up some of their own desires in order to please parents and other adults. This should be accomplished with as little frustration as possible.

Play assumes two important functions in relation to developing behavioral controls. It enables children to act out some of the frustrations they feel in learning to accept limitations on their behavior. And, it provides the arena in which children begin to exercise self-control.

Much learning must occur between preschool years and adulthood when one is expected to function effectively in situations in which one must exercise considerable control. Much of this early learning occurs because of the careful guidance of parents and teachers. Even in families where the limits are reasonable, young children experience much frustration and disappointment when they are not allowed to do what they want to. They express some of this frustration through crying and direct hostility, but some of it is expressed much more subtly through play. Most teachers have seen "young mothers" spank their dolls almost to the point of being abusive. It happens so often that teachers do not think much about it. They do not assume that the particular child has been spanked, only that, for this child, abusing the doll could be a legitimate form of release and does not need to be punished. Children, acting in the role of someone else, can do things that they would not be allowed to do themselves. They would be stopped from hitting or spanking another person.

Some release from frustration also occurs when children engage in other energy-release forms of play, such as gross motor activities, carpentry, use of various art media especially fingerpaint and clay, and water play. In play, they can pound, squeeze, pour, and smear. They can also make a grand and glorious mess. Some children have already become so controlled by three or four years old that they will not play with anything that is wet, messy, or dirty, but a more typical reaction at this age is one of freedom and enjoyment. They spread paint around, mix all the colors together, and pour and spill water without an apparent care. Having a place where messy materials can legitimately be used helps them to accept the controls that must be exercised in other settings. The use of play as a corrective activity will be discussed in detail in Chapter Eight, therefore, it is only mentioned here.

During preschool years when children first engage in sociodramatic play, they have a limited number of opportunities to exercise self-discipline, because they are still in the process of learning to conform to the standards set for them by adults. They are concerned with maintaining good relationships with their parents and other adults yet they sometimes abide by their own wishes.

In sociodramatic play, when other children impose the rules, they are not able to do and say exactly what they want and remain a part of the play. Whatever roles children assume, they must project the essence of the role. If not, they are criticized or ignored by their peers, and the role may be taken away. This requires children to limit and select actions in order to portray clearly the main characteristics of their roles. Not only must children learn to concentrate on a role, but they must also learn to concentrate on the theme of the play episode. If children do not concentrate on the group perception of the theme, other children will demand that they leave the group and the role be assumed by someone else. Part of the value of this concentration is that it is enforced by playmates instead of by a parent or teacher. Because they are forced to make choices between concentrating on the role or leaving the play, children learn to discipline themselves to do what the play requires. So long as children handle these situations with reasonable fairness, you do not need to intervene. However, when children are unfairly rejected or continuously denied the opportunity to play, you may have to intervene in their behalf and help work through the situation more fairly and reasonably. However, children usually get the point and modify their behavior in order to play without adult intervention.

For children in the six to eight-year-old range, learning about rules is also helpful in developing behavioral controls. There is something about a rule that makes it special. One is supposed to conform, and if children won't "play fair," they will be ejected from the group, usually after much quarreling. Of course, with younger children, the rules may change momentarily but that does not seem to matter. These children may be able to solve their own problems during playground games, but with card games, counting games, and other supposedly quieter games, the presence of an older child or adult can help keep things running more smoothly, because they usually reinforce behavior which is in accordance with the rules.

We are only beginning to understand the contribution of sociodramatic play to the mastery of the social environment. Fortunately, as a teacher you do not have to understand every value that play may have, but you do have to be sensitive to the child's use of play in order to provide the props and guidance needed. A part of this sensitivity includes knowing when to intervene and when to just be watchful. Every child has to work toward understanding and mastering the social environment. Other children and adults can assist in ways that are supportive and satisfying.

NOTES

1. Sara Smilansky, *The Effects of Sociodramatic Play on Disadvantaged Preschool Children,* (New York, New York: John Wiley and Sons, Inc., 1968), p. 9.

2. Eleanor Pavenstedt et al., *The Drifters. Children of Disorganized Families* (Boston: Little Brown, 1967), 345 pp.

3. Sara Smilansky, pp. 1–164.

4. Robert D. Hess et al., *The Cognitive Environments of Urban Preschool Children, Final Report* (Chicago: the Graduate School of Education, University of Chicago, 1968), 381 pp.

5. Joan T. Freyburg, *The Enhancement of Fantasy Ability in Lower-Class Kindergarten Children* (Ph.D. Thesis, City University of New York, 1969).

6. Brian Sutton-Smith, *Play as Variability Training and, As the Useless made Useful* (ERIC ED 084008), 1972, 10 p.

7. Sara Smilansky, p. 27.

8. Sara Smilansky, pp. 28–31.

CHAPTER
FIVE

*Increased social contact during reproductive play
helps the child reproduce social realities.*

Developing
As an Individual

Children's Individuality

Certain aspects of individuality can be observed during the early months of life, although the full flowering of one's uniqueness continues throughout life. Individuality affects development, of course, in the areas already considered (see Chapters Three and Four) understanding and mastering the physical and social environment. Further, individuality is reflected in the child's creative and recreational activities, as we will show in Chapter Six. We will discuss some of the common influences of the child's individuality on these other areas of development incidentally in this chapter. But we will concern ourselves primarily with how individuality develops in relation to play and how to foster such development through play.

However, let us examine first what is meant by "developing as an individual." What we immediately think of is how children view themselves as persons. We will use the term *self identity* to refer to this aspect of individuality. Self identity includes children's understanding of who they are individually, their

feelings about themselves, and gradual recognition of personal characteristics, such as temperament and abilities, which in their unique combination
within the individual child help to define personality.

Other aspects of the development of individuality include children's
human equipment for interacting with the physical environment, and the rate
at which and the extent to which, children develop use of this equipment.
They develop feelings about the self in response to how and how much they
have developed the use of their human equipment. By *human equipment*
we mean: the body as a balanced and coordinated implement of action; the
sensory and manipulative abilities used to explore and construct; and the
capacity to regulate through attention one's exploration, construction, and
other action.

Individuality develops during early childhood in two additional ways: preferences for people, places, activities, roles, and objects; and the real or
imaginary sources of children's emotional concerns, as well as the styles
they use in dealing with their own concerns.

Now that we have in view an overall conception of these aspects of
individuality, we can consider the role of play in the development of each
of them.

Aspects of Individuality

Self Identity—Who the Child Is. All areas of self identity follow a generally
uniform developmental pattern. The growing personal sense in children of
who they are is illustrative of these developmental steps. In infancy children
discover themselves as separate from others; their inner sense of desire or
longing (motivation) helps them to recognize personal identity. In infancy
children also discover themselves as causes of what happens in their small
world. During the period of productive play, young preschoolers come more
fully to understand their wills against the background of their parents' allowing
or restraining actions and words. Thus, "no" becomes a central focus for
both children and adults. Children, within the bounds of permitted activity,
produce what they desire and thereby learn who they are in terms of what
they are allowed to do. However, they are learning more than simply what
is allowed; they are learning: "I can do this" and "I can do it all by myself."
During the period of reproductive play, children's focus of action shifts to
constructing and to matching to reality whatever they produce. "Who I am"
now means viewing oneself in terms of role possibilities encountered at home
and in the immediate neighborhood. It also begins to mean their identification
with the products they produce.

During the primary school years, the self is increasingly identified in terms
of the groups to which one belongs: "I am a nine-year-old girl in the fourth
grade, and I am the oldest child in my whole family, so I am also the oldest
of all the grandchildren in my family. My parents both work and we live in

a nice house." This relates fairly directly to the notion of games with rules; children now view the self in terms of social definitions on which there is some general consensus. In a similar manner, children adopt the social perceptions of the school environment and begin to view self in terms of either *(a)* developing skills and potentialities, or *(b)* matching their performance to that of their classmates. The first of these perspectives may be adopted in classrooms having an "individually guided progress" orientation; the latter perspective may come from classrooms emphasizing the more competitive aspects of achievement.

How then does play contribute to children's emerging sense of self? Depending upon the developmental stage, play which most typifies the children's ages provides focus into the most helpful forms of developmental activity. In general, in reviewing the preceding paragraph we can conclude that whatever facilitates the developmental task indicated is beneficial. For example, for youngsters who have moved into productive play, being confronted with only necessary and clearly defined limits by parents should facilitate their development of a sense of self, allowing them to do and accomplish a variety of things. Therefore, at the most general level, the teacher can be guided by the generalizations which flow from the beginning of this section regarding what will facilitate children's development of a sense of self at each age.

More specific ideas can also be considered for relating play to the need to develop a sense of self during the preschool and primary years. Playing with a "family doll set" helps many youngsters to explore their place within their family, and if other children are involved with them in the same play, they can also learn about other families. For these reasons it is desirable to have more than one family doll set in a classroom and to have sufficient child dolls to represent the various child members. The most commonly available doll sets from commercial sources do not provide the desirable number of boy and girl dolls of different ages, and few sets include adults other than parents. One recent development has been the manufacture of doll sets to represent various racial groups; older sets provided only white-skinned dolls. These racial variations are desirable in most early childhood programs, even when the children are nearly all from the same group racially. The experience of playing with racially different and racially similar families of dolls can contribute to children's capacity for understanding through play how racially different families might handle common domestic situations. Because children's story books and family television programming now provide racially different models, children of various backgrounds may desire to play out themes involving persons who differ from themselves.

To overcome the limitations of commercially available doll sets, especially for use by children who are a little older, child and adult figures of different ages and racial backgrounds can be cut out of expired mail order catalogs. These catalogs can also provide some household furnishings. If these figures are premounted on heavy paper or lightweight cardboard, they will last longer and can be handled almost like dolls. A plastic or lacquer coating will preserve the printed surface through a lot of handling. If time cannot be taken to mount these cutouts, they can be used on an inclined (i.e., somewhat more horizontal than vertical) flannel board where they will retain the locations assigned to them by the children. Yarn can be used on the flannel to outline rooms; younger children will need some help either setting these figures up initially or accepting their limitations and fragility compared to dolls. Cutting out the figures is best accomplished by using a broad outline; older children can help cut them out if precision outlines are not emphasized.

Household play in the housekeeping area provides all of the same potentials as dolls for exploring one's place in the family. But the two situations require really different kinds of imagination. Less mature children may be able to explore family relations with the dolls, but lack the more advanced verbal skills required to sustain a similar interaction with other children. Because young children usually play best at sociodramatic play in very small groups, the potential for including a large family of characters in household play is limited at any given time. Household play, however, does provide more opportunity for give and take, which may assist those children whose family relations are centered around issues of interpersonal conflict and accommodation.

Adult guidance during both doll play and household play can assist children to sharpen their questions, clarify issues, and explore alternative courses of action within the family. Many suggestions for noncontrolling adult interventions in sociodramatic play will be found in Chapter Four, and can be readily applied to the issue of children's places within the family. It will of course be important to move into such interventions by following the child, i.e., by introducing only conceptions which the child seems ready to receive. Even children who are having problems relative to their place in the family (e.g., children from families experiencing serious sibling rivalry or from families where some important person has been lost to the family) can usually benefit from exploring alternative courses of action. The teacher, by participating in doll play, can model for the children more successful ways of handling interpersonal conflict; the method is to show how it is done successfully—not to tell the children nor to direct them to try it another way.

The development of self identity also advances when children become more sure of their own body boundaries. Play with mirrors can help children to clarify where their various body parts are when they assume particular postures and gestures, are involved in performing a given action, or are experiencing and expressing an emotional state. Thus, a mirror is useful in the household area. Having more than one mirror may be essential at times. Dolls are helpful also for children who are studying body boundaries. The children may need teacher assistance in learning the names of various body parts. Parts which are less familiar to them can be learned by the teacher's participatory emphasis (not to be confused with drill) on the less known parts. For example, the teacher might inquire in a typical "accident victim" play situation, "Are you sure you hurt only your leg? It looked like you bumped your backbone too. Let's check to see if your backbone was injured." Soon the children will gain familiarity with elbow, shoulder, kneecap, and cheekbone in this manner. Greater familiarity with body parts may thus begin to contribute to their overall sense of the body as the center of the self.

Finally, how children handle themselves in situations where others challenge their rights or territory has a bearing on the sense of self. A healthy sense of self means asserting one's rights without malice toward other children who intrude into the child's personal space. During free play, this means that the teacher will allow and even encourage, if necessary, children's assertion of rights. Generally, the children will be encouraged to settle their own differences, but when serious and persistent examples occur of one child intruding upon another's rights, the teacher should become involved to guide and even restrain if necessary. Standing near to offer moral support is usually sufficient to encourage timid children to assert themselves. A group game, which can encourage children to recognize each other's rights, goes as follows: children take turns serving as group leader who directs the group to perform various actions ("Simon Says" is one form of the game); the teacher helps the leader child to "catch" those who do not accurately carry out the instructions, with those who best follow them being the winners. It is best, for this purpose, to have the actions remain simple so that most children will have no difficulty performing them, leaving, as the only issue, the one of following another child's directions. Many children will naturally get into situations of this sort during sociodramatic play, and the teacher will find it least cumbersome to encourage the children to assert themselves in this context.

Feelings About the Self. This section considers the positive versus negative feelings or appraisals that children make regarding themselves. Producing positive self concepts in children within realistic limits of self perception, is a central goal of most early childhood programs. How a child's self image becomes positive is no real mystery. Children who are wanted, loved, and enjoyed, who are assisted in developing their competencies, and who are not subjected to excessive frustration are the children who have positive and realistic self concepts. Usually, too, children who learn to take care of their own needs, such as feeding, toileting, and dressing feel more positive about themselves. It will, therefore, come as no surprise that many children enter their preschool or school experience already having either primarily positive or primarily negative feelings about themselves as a result of prior experiences. What teachers often fail to realize is how easily these feelings may be changed in either direction by new experiences while the children are young. School experience can change children's self feelings, or it can confirm the feelings they already have. Young children usually let us know how they feel about themselves when they are involved in play, so play is a point of contact with these important feelings. By observing play, the teacher can see how children's self feelings are progressing. The most realistic place to help children in play is in the provision of materials to meet their developmental interests and needs. By having these available and providing them as needed, the teacher can protect children from being frustrated. The unavailability of appropriate materials or, sometimes, the availability of almost appropriate materials which attract the children's interest but are too sophisticated or demanding for them can be equally as frustrating. And of course the teacher can accept, love, and enjoy each child, taking pleasure in the children's own desire to master what before has eluded them. These general considerations are more suited to helping children develop positive self concepts than are specific forms of play. Further assistance in finding a good match of materials to children's developmental needs is available from Chapters Two and Seven, which consider, respectively, the issues and challenges experienced in play at different developmental levels, and the selection of materials to meet play needs at different age levels.

Recognition of Personal Characteristics. Realization of personal characteristics comes only gradually and incompletely during early childhood. In fact, adults are still in the process of learning about themselves in this area. Nevertheless, young children can and do learn much about their individual uniqueness through participation in an early childhood program. As children take on different roles in dramatic play, some roles appeal to them more than others. As they participate in sociodramatic play, the other children find a particular child more imaginative and hence more believable in particular roles. In response to the greater ease with which individual children perform certain roles, they adopt these and partially identify with them. In turn, children come to think of themselves in terms of the roles which they successfully play: "When I grow up I'm going to be a _____," serves as a reminder of how easily children move from what they perceive as a possible role for themselves to thinking of themselves as becoming that kind of person when they grow up.

Teachers also find many opportunities to comment to individual children about their observations of what the children do well and what they enjoy doing. These observations are gleaned from any and all aspects of play. Children respond by remembering and perhaps incorporating these observations into their concept of themselves. In the future, children who have been thus stimulated may have occasion to think of themselves in these ways: "I can run very fast," "I always like to feed the fish," "I take such good care of the baby when we play house," "I get excited real easy when there's something funny or scarey happening," "My skin's so sensitive that I can even feel when the wind blows a tiny bit," "I'm getting to know my numbers real good," "Teacher thinks I talk just like you, Mom!" References to the self are never incidental or unimportant to children. They treasure the kind things that are said about them, and usually they remember them longer than the mean things they may sometimes hear. The teacher who remembers this and who is a careful observer will find occasion from time to time to add realistic, positive "treasures" to the children's self perceptions. Lest the teacher feel reluctant to pass along such observations, it is well to remember that we can be open to hearing many truths about ourselves from someone who accepts us, whereas we may not be open to learning these things from someone who makes the same observation in the form of an accusation. The teacher who accepts children and freely expresses that acceptance is in a very favored position to help the children become accurate and positive observers of themselves.

Temperament. There are areas of personal development which most children do not recognize as such during the preschool and primary years. Temperament is probably the most influential of these on children's development. We will use the word *temperament* to refer to how children do things rather than to the particular things they do. That is, *temperament* refers to the personal style in which the child characteristically behaves. Temperament reveals itself as a style across all areas of behavior; it is not a specific form of behavior.

Some aspects of temperament which can readily be inferred by observing young children at play are:

(a) how actively they perform most behaviors
(b) whether their mood is usually more pleasant or unpleasant
(c) whether they generally tend to approach or to avoid new experiences
(d) the degree of persistence which they display in continuing to do what they are already doing or how long they continue an activity if uninterrupted
(e) how strong a stimulus is required before they show some reaction
(f) how intensely they react when they have experienced a stimulus
(g) how easily and readily they adapt to new or changed situations
(h) the extent to which they are distracted by stimuli that are unrelated to their ongoing activities.

A final aspect of temperament is not so easily inferred by teachers, although parents are usually familiar with this facet of their children's styles. It is the regularity or rhythm of the child's physical functions, such as appetite, elimination from bowel and bladder, alertness or wakefulness, and sleep or rest. Some children are irregular and others are more regular or predictable in these functions.[1]

Temperament is a fairly constant or unchanging aspect of the self from infancy onward. We do not, therefore, expect children's temperaments to change. But we can expect that children, who receive thoughtful and caring guidance, will become increasingly able to behave effectively within the range of their individual temperaments. And they will become increasingly able to capitalize upon their temperamental strengths.

The teacher's first activities in relation to children's temperaments will be to recognize and accept them. This also means not trying to change them. Then the teacher can build upon this foundation by helping children through play to find effective ways of behaving and of structuring their own environments in line with their own temperaments.

The teacher will, for example, recognize and accept the highly active dispositions of some children, and will not mistakenly label temperamentally active children as "hyperactive." Most active children are simply that, active children. Active children usually need a little more individual space for whatever they are doing. Teachers will therefore give attention to providing sufficient space and spacing. It really helps.

If some of the children are easily stimulated by others' activities, and especially if they are intense in their reactions to being stimulated, providing sufficient space and spacing for the active ones will help the reactive children as well. Some very intensely reactive children will need to be somewhat insulated or bufferred. For example, they may do better in a developmental activity area where walls, screen dividers, and carpeting tend to lower the total amount of noise, movement, and other stimulation reaching them.

Children who usually avoid new experiences may just need time to overcome their initial reluctance. But additional time will help only if they are also given repeated exposures to the new experiences. Play can provide a nonthreatening context into which to introduce the same experiences repeatedly until the child can deal with them.

Lines of reasoning similar to those already presented may be applied to each of the other aspects of temperament. Eventually, as children gain familiarity with how you are helping them to cope within the framework of their individual temperaments, you can do something more. You can begin to share with them the wisdom and success of your own observations about how they can maintain optimal conditions for themselves. You might mention to one child, for instance, "I've noticed that Tommy likes you a lot, but that he gets upset if you play too close to him when he's trying to finish something. Yesterday you asked him if he wanted to play and he said, 'Pretty soon.' So you waited a little while longer. Then he *was* ready to play," or "Have you noticed that when you leave your wraps on you get very warm and uncomfortable? But when you take them off, you start to feel better and to have fun again." In this way you can help the children to begin to understand and apply information about (a) their impacts on other children as a function of the other children's temperaments, and (b) their own temperament-related reactions. Going yet another step, you can help children to begin to anticipate such reactions and to use successful ways of dealing with them. It is important to observe that none of these suggestions calls for you to encourage children to change their temperaments.

Children's Own Human Equipment

The Body As Implement of Action. Learning about one's individuality in this area begins very early after children have mastered the fundamentals of creeping, and later, walking and running. Even learning these skilled acts of motion adds something to children's sense of mastery by making them feel that they are masters of their own bodies. When children are very young, adults help by keeping the immediate environment clear of dangerous objects so that the children can freely use their bodies to explore. Since many injuries result during the early years from exceeding one's physical limits, supervision is essential to safety. Adults further contribute to body mastery by providing children with equipment that is suitable, challenging, and safe for large muscle development. Developmental level is a prime consideration in deciding what is suitable, challenging, and safe. The guidelines provided by Chapter Seven for equipment selection will be extremely useful in this connection as you consider decisions about tricycles, swings, slides, and climbing apparatus.

Gross motor learning through play is not restricted to interactions with physical equipment. Much of this learning takes place during early rough and tumble social play, running the whole gambit from catch through tag and hide and seek. In sociodramatic play, proper role performance often calls for skilled use of the whole body in a convincing show of poised balance and coordination. In addition to the formal team games of the primary school years, children learn from keep-away, kick-the-can, dodge ball, statues, crack the whip, and from increasingly demanding equipment including parallel ladder, cross bar, bicycle, scooter, sled, and skates.

Underlying the joy of personal control of the body at all levels, is an element of excitement associated with the rapid stimulation of the body's balance mechanism concealed and protected in the inner ear. This element is present when young children beg parents to twirl them around more, or when children turn rapidly in circles until dizzy. Preschool age children achieve similar sensations from rapid and high sailing in the swing, rushing down a steep slide, balancing near the top of the climbing apparatus, or going faster and faster on the merry-go-round. Primary level children achieve similar sensations from climbing trees and from a host of carnival and amusement park type rides. These rides undoubtedly substitute in the lives of modern children for the excitement formerly experienced in first hunts and trips to dangerous or "spirit-inhabited" places. Thus, it is well to see that body mastery is balance and coordination plus the pleasure that comes from rapid stimulation or exposure to risk and danger, immediately followed by a return to equilibrium and safety. It will come then as no surprise that body mastery activities often court danger. The teacher who is willing to face the implications of this fact will realize that a certain sense of danger and overstimulation may be essential to most limit-testing forms of large motor mastery. The trick is to preserve the children's access to the sensation of overstimulation without undue exposure to the risk of injury. The teacher must figuratively tightrope walk to preserve the children's sometimes almost literal tightrope walk. The teacher's tightrope act balances between these two dangers: being heedless of the children's safety and becoming a killjoy, safety addict.

Remembering individual differences can bring some sanity back to this process. Children of the same age may have achieved quite different degrees of physical mastery and may therefore require quite contrasting degrees of stimulating activity to challenge them. One can usually allow greater latitude of physical risk to those children who are capable of handling it. The teacher must be alert to accident prone children and provide an added margin of safety through guidance and direct supervision. Yet above all these considerations, it is well to remember that even very physically competent children can have "high risk days" and are not to be overlooked when they excessively tax their own limits or the law of gravity. And all children become a bit more accident prone when excessively tired, ill, emotionally out of sorts, hungry, or otherwise overdriven.

Sensory and Manipulative Abilities. These abilities begin developing in infancy when infants hear their parents' voices, look at their faces, and feel their touch while parents feed and clothe them. The mouth also works as a sensory and exploratory organ at this age. By the primary level, children understand and use with ease all the basic sounds and much of the vocabulary and syntax of adult language. Hand and eye, which at first would not work together, have become coordinated to the extent that children begin producing written language. A marvelous transformation has been wrought by now in children's capacities to sense and process information, to use hand and eye to explore and solve new mysteries, and to use hand and eye to construct things of beauty and usefulness. And all of this has come about in the first seven to eight years of their lives. Whenever we encounter such rapid and profound developmental changes, during a period so dominated by play as is early childhood, we may be certain that play has shaped the children's sensory and manipulative progress in manifold ways. An entire book might easily be devoted to the examination of these abilities and play's contributions to them.

Most of the important sounds which children are trying to master occur in human speech. Teachers and other adults assist children in this process by speaking clearly while adapting their language to the children's level of understanding during the early years. In the classroom, a relatively quiet atmosphere permits children to hear more clearly what is said to them. If this is coupled with activity and interest center arrangement of the room, children will find themselves fairly undistracted in an interesting location where materials will stimulate their curiosity and desire to play. Children will often talk freely in this kind of setting, conversing with other children who may be interested in hearing what the individual child has to say especially if the teacher is near. It is natural to talk and to listen under these conditions. For those children who have special needs in this area of sensory development, further assistance can be provided through a variety of simple, sound discrimination games. For example, the teacher can teach the children to clap their hands to match the teacher's rate or to musical rhythm. Then the children can be asked to clap faster or slower or louder or softer. Each variation is continued in the form of a responsive game. With older children, pitch variations can be used in a singing or humming voice. If singing, "la la la" works well for sample note presentations.

Visual discrimination will develop whenever children engage in a variety of manipulative activities using many media. Visual discrimination, as well as concept development, will be furthered if the teacher can draw the children's attention to various sensory qualities available to be experienced: "See how dark this color is," "I'll try to make a wavy line that looks like yours," "I notice how much you like to use red and blue together when you paint." The possibilities here are almost limitless, so long as these teacher comments are made naturally in the context of what the children are doing. Touch or tactile discrimination can be promoted in the same way. Both visual and tactile discrimination of objects may also be tried. (i.e., In contrast to simple discrimination of sensory qualities, children may be allowed to encounter new objects such as plants and soils at a touch table or experience bench.) Another variation of this which some children enjoy is trying to recognize objects visually which are partly concealed (e.g., the familiar "I spy" game) or to recognize objects by touch which are completely concealed from view, such as in a "feel sack." Children can learn to play all of these games with one another. They love to see whether they can pick something difficult for another child to guess.

Manipulative abilities can be furthered by providing in the classroom for sensory play, constructive play, and a variety of creative artwork activities, depending on the ages and needs of the individual children. Beyond making these provisions, we generally do not advocate an active role for the teacher. Most of the teacher interventions during these activities are recommended for reasons other than promoting the development of manipulative skills. For a more complete treatment of suitable manipulative materials, see Chapter Seven. It is enough to note here that blocks of all types, specially made construction toy sets, peg and nail boards, looms, tools, and all kinds of art materials are useful, and most of them can be used in a variety of ways depending upon the children's developmental levels and inclinations. Among the manipulative skills for which you should make provision are construction, copying, and drawing. All can potentially be performed in a great variety of media. A final type of manipulative activity which is especially challenging to primary age children is the manipulative puzzle, such as those made of curiously interlocking metal pieces which can be separated in only one way, or the miniature wooden objects made up of interlocking pieces of varied, irregular shape. A trick puzzle corner in the room will occupy some children for considerable time while challenging their manipulative and problem solving abilities.

Regulation of Attention. The ability to regulate attention grows directly out of the foregoing types of sensory and manipulative activity. Ability to regulate attention also grows out of the active use of imagination in play. Play therefore offers much to children for the development of attentional control. And higher order cognitive skills such as planning, initiating, and persisting in action relate closely to and depend upon attention. Ordinarily it will be enough if the teacher provides the kinds of materials already mentioned for sensory and manipulative play, plus those discussed in Chapters Four and Seven for dramatic and other imaginative play. For some children whose attentional regulation does not develop as readily through forms of play, attention building games may be used. Simon Says is one such game; many more can readily be devised by the teacher for auditory attention. For visual attention, the game Rock-Scissors-Paper may be helpful, as may Follow the Leader if finer behavioral details are emphasized.

In summary, children's human equipment and its development comprise an important aspect of the child's individuality. We have examined *(a)* the body as an implement of action, *(b)* the child's sensory and manipulative abilities, and *(c)* attentional regulation as areas within the child's physical individuality.

Development of Preferences

By the primary level, children's preferences, perhaps more than any other aspect of individuality, set the individual child apart from all others as unique. Preferences develop through the early childhood years for particular objects, people, activities, places, and roles. A preference develops following a successful or rewarding interaction with any one of the previously mentioned classes, such as objects. After an initially successful interaction, children attempt to repeat the interaction at a future time. These repeated attempts to approach or interact are what we call preferences. There are also those things which are negatively preferred; that is, the child has not had a successful or rewarding history of experience with them and consequently avoids or otherwise seeks not to interact with them.

The goal of early childhood education in this aspect of development is that children shall become able to have preferences, and further, that these preferences shall be rather encompassing instead of limited or narrow. Often, having preferences is directly equated by some educators with making choices. It would be truer to say that choices are made on the basis of preferences than to suggest that making choices creates preferences or the ability to have varied preferences. To state accurately the conditions which produce the "ability to have varied preferences," we need to include some reference to the previously described process of preference development. Such a statement might look like this: to have the capacity for wide and varied preferences (and, hence, choices), children need to have varied experiences in which the probability of successful or rewarding interaction is high.

Therefore, to promote development of the ability for wide and varied preferences, the teacher will need to provide for the child varied experiences with objects, people, activities, places, and roles in such a way that the children will be able to interact successfully or rewardingly with them. To promote preferences it is not necessary to provide choices, but to promote choices it is necessary to provide preferences. Relying on choices alone will often only guarantee that the children will continue to choose what they already prefer; it will not of necessity (in fact probably will not) lead to the formation of many new preferences. Put another way, children continue to be attracted to what already attracts them—unless adults make special provisions for other outcomes.

How then can the teacher promote new preferences through play? By introducing into the play environment previously neutral objects and activities, which have been carefully selected to match the current developmental capacities of the children for interacting with them successfully. Arranging the environment in the manner long advocated by John Dewey is then the key to developing the preferential aspect of individuality.

Children's Emotional Concerns

Emotional concerns is the final aspect of individuality development which we will consider here. Emotional concerns arise of course out of children's experiences. The major emotional concerns relate further to the primary issues or tasks of emotional and social development. During play we see, as it were, a "royal road to the child's unconscious." That is to say, play reflects in symbolic form at times, and in enactive forms at other times, the essential emotional concerns of individual children. Considerably more attention will be given to the use of play to resolve emotional concerns when we consider therapeutic uses of play in Chapter Eight; thus, much of what can be said is reserved for later discussion. In the present context, it will be sufficient to recognize that emotional concerns appear in play *when* suitable play opportunities are provided. Now it is unlikely that any preschool program will be managed so inappropriately as to preclude children dealing with their emotional concerns through play, although it seems altogether likely that some primary level programs will make no provision for these concerns. It is small wonder, in view of this, that emotional concerns often interfere with school learning at the primary level—and that the same concerns continue to exert a detrimental effect upon children's school learning year after year without ever being resolved. Study after study has indicated that a third or more of all children in the "normal" school population are significantly, behaviorally disturbed throughout the primary school years.[2] We attempt in Chapter Nine to imagine a new and believable kind of school where some of the problems of current public education would largely disappear.

But even without getting into the therapeutic side of play, the teacher can make provision for children's emotional concerns to be expressed and worked upon in the context of play. These are the essentials:

(a) provision will be made for developmentally meaningful play as advocated throughout this text
(b) teachers will provide guidance and resources to meet individual needs

(c) adult supervision will assure safety and protection if necessary

(d) the individuality of children will be accepted, encouraged, and promoted as discussed throughout this chapter.

We can be sure that the teacher and classroom that provide these essentials will make it possible for children to deal with emotional concerns. This will be enough for the majority of behaviorally disturbed children. Only a small portion of these children will need special provision of therapeutic play measures.

NOTES

1. We are especially indebted to Thomas, Chess, and Birch for their careful study and definition of children's temperament. In addition to several published articles, a primary reference for their work is: Alexander Thomas *et al., Temperament and Behavior Disorders in Children* (New York, New York: New York University Press, 1968).

2. Harvey F. Clarizio and George F. McCoy, *Behavior Disorders in Children,* 2nd. Edition (New York, New York: Thomas Y. Crowell Co., 1976), Chapter 3.

CHAPTER

SIX

*Work with malleable materials develops
imaginations and encourages creativity.*

Creating
and Recreating

Fantasy and imagination are important elements in development. Although the two elements are often considered to be identical, we shall describe how they function and how they differ, especially in relation to creativity and the creative aspects of life. Fantasy and imagination are vital not only in childhood but also later in the development of creative adults. That is, adults who have imagination and and those with problem solving abilities necessary for survival are known to have several characteristics which probably originate in early childhood.

In addition to fantasy and imagination, this chapter also considers the development of games and recreational activities. Many people are concerned that we, as adults, do not know how to enjoy ourselves and use our leisure time for personal profit and well being. The need for exercise and continued physical activity is also a contemporary concern. The final section of this chapter examines a closely related area, tension release through play.

Fantasy

Fantasy is an important part of the child's life. Through fantasy the child learns to cope with his surroundings and comes to understand his world. We see this in many aspects of the child's life, for example, the way in which a child plays with a doll. If you watch a child playing, with dolls, he will reveal his feelings about a new baby in the home, or show how he wants to be treated, or how he has seen one of his parents or some other adult treat a baby. If he is not frustrated, you will probably see him "practicing" what he has seen. If he is frustrated you will see him working out his feelings and frustrations. In this way he learns how to express his feelings as well as when to suppress some feelings. It is, therefore, a very necessary part of the growth process.

Fantasy includes daydreaming which is controlled by the individual's desires. For this reason daydreaming was considered undesirable by some early psychologists and educators. Modern psychology has recognized, however, the healthy function fantasy plays in the child's life and has determined that fantasy is linked with the more complex processes of the human mind, such as creativity and problem solving.

The infant, or preverbal child, has no way of distinguishing fantasy from reality. We have no way of truly identifying what is happening in the mind of such a young child, but Piaget's observational methods of early mental processes helps us observe the process. All the experiences children have interweave with each other in feelings, pictures (mental imagery), and imagination. At the earliest age, children have no words to express feelings and experiences, but gradually they begin to connect words to concepts and experiences.

Words, in the beginning, are related to names of objects and people. Children accompany much of their play with speech by age three. Because they talk while they play, we can tell what they are doing from the standpoint of the child. At this stage most play and talking about play is functional or productive. That is, play is still very repetitive and acts as practice for learning about the environment or for developing certain skills. Make believe is simple, because the imagination is very limited.

Another aspect of fantasy is that it involves things as subjectively experienced or perceived (and hence potentially not decentered) rather than things as might appear to an "objective" observer. A more complete definition of fantasy described by levels through which a child develops is available in our earlier book, *Early Childhood Programs: Developmental Objectives and their Use.*[1] Overall definitional material on creativity is also available.

How the Child Uses Fantasy Play

From the age of three the child is very involved in fantasy play. Many perceptions up to the age of eight or nine are entirely fantasy. Experiences are interwoven with stories and pictures from books, television, movies, and other media. And, of course, by age eight or nine the child's verbal language has vastly increased. The child can verbalize and discuss experiences and fantasies or express feelings and ideas verbally. We can often pinpoint conflicts between fantasy and reality by what we hear the child saying. When we watch a child of three or four line up toy animals or dolls and tell them what they must do to be friends, we realize that the child would probably like to do this with peers or siblings. The child can also see that trying this with other children, produces rejection, and the child realizes that people cannot be controlled.

Children may not, on the other hand, realize that there is a conflict between reality and fantasy. In fact, this is often our clue as to where they are in their thinking processes. Young children, ages two and three, consider external elements to be very real. Just the way they describe natural elements, such as where the sun goes at night or where the stars are during the day, gives us some indication as to what they are thinking. Natural elements are often greeted as people. The two-year-old can be observed saying, "Hi, lake," "Hi, moon," as though greeting an old friend.

Just listening to children often does not tell us what concepts they actually have. One or two words cannot be precise enough to indicate just how much the child understands. Thus, it is difficult to determine how the child is differentiating between fantasy and reality. It is sometimes possible to tell by watching the play develop, but even then it is not always possible to be absolutely sure as to its meaning. Piaget's observational methods are helpful in determining meaning.

Without words to describe all that is going on in their minds, children turn to play to express fantasies and imaginative thoughts. They use whatever appropriate materials are available for this expression. They combine these elements in ways that show their understanding. One three-year-old, for example, was fascinated with his father's guitar. One day he brought a guitar home from nursery school which he had made himself. It consisted of a four inch piece of wood approximately one and one-half inches wide with three small nails on each end. Rubber bands were stretched over the nails to form the "guitar strings." He showed his parents how it worked and was very satisfied with the sound of the rubber bands. It did not bother him that the quality of the sound was poor or that a real guitar has six strings. He had expressed his feelings about "his guitar" satisfactorily for his level of understanding.

At the preschool and kindergarten level, children can be satisfied with representations when adults would feel uncomfortable without words or precise illustrations. A three-year-old drew a map one day of the route his mother took to drive him to school. When he showed the drawing to his teacher, she observed a series of dots and lines on a piece of manilla paper. She asked him to tell her about it, and the child, who was very verbal, was able to describe and explain what most of the dots on the map meant. The line represented the streets his mother followed, the dots represented schools, churches, a water tower, and other landmarks which they passed along the streets. This child was perhaps better able to describe what was in his head than many three's. For this reason, you should always recognize that although it may be impossible for children to describe their work, it *does have meaning* for the individual child and should be respected and acknowledged.

We often see examples of how the meaning moves in the child's mind in easel painting. Bright red and orange can represent a raging fire with all the fire fighting going on in the child's thinking. Eventually, the final product may end up muddy gray, or even black, representing the end of the fire. Unless you observe the total process the child has gone through while making the painting, you may not appreciate the final black or muddy gray product.

As language facility increases, the kind and the intensity of play decreases. Whereas preschoolers, for example, talk almost constantly as they play with toy cars and trucks, the older children talk less. Younger children may use words to describe actions although older children simply initiate conversation between drivers. In fact, the decrease in the intensity of play reaches a point where in adulthood some people allow no time for play in their lives. For those who do, it can be a significant factor in their lives and in certain aspects a motivating force.

Value of Fantasy Play

Fantasy play serves a variety of purposes. One is to act out wishful thinking. When children imagine themselves to be Daniel Boone or Isis, they are satisfying an inner desire to be someone different, or they are experimenting to find out how it feels to be a super something. Acting openly and within the context of the play situation, they can learn the limits of reality. They learn they cannot fly like Isis or fight like Daniel Boone, at least not without getting hurt. Children learn quickly that all of the hitting on television shows is painful when imitated in real life.

An example of the child discovering reality through fantasy play was observed in a two and one-half-year-old boy who was a Popeye cartoon fan. His mother dressed him in a snow suit and let him go outside to play in the snow. He fell backwards in a snowdrift and in the confining snow suit could not get up. He immediately went through the motions "Popeye" uses just before he does some phenomenal feat. He was very surprised to find that this did not raise him out of the snowdrift and could not understand why it did not work for him.

Children also learn that reality limits behavior. They can fantasize what they would do to someone with whom they are angry like tearing off an arm. In their minds this action is not bad or even permanent because the arm can just as quickly be "put back on." But when they tear an arm off a doll or stuffed animal, they learn that it can not easily be put back on. In these kinds of experiences, children gradually come to realize the boundaries between fantasy and reality.

In fantasy play, fantasy and reality temper each other. Without reality, a world of fantasy can be chaotic. Likewise, a world without fantasy would be harsh and cold. Life is more balanced and full when the two elements are integrated. Adult day dreaming is a process resembling childhood fantasizing.

Although fantasy play begins before age five, it is fuller, richer, and more often expressed verbally in children over the age of five. After age five, children can easily slip from fantasy to reality and back again. They are aware of the difference in many instances, especially if role playing is involved. While they can completely submerge themselves in a role, they can just as quickly become themselves again when the situation demands it. In this sense, the child's use of fantasy differs from an adult's use of it as a means of escaping from the seemingly impossible reality of the present. In fantasy play, children older than five usually know the difference between the fantasy involved in the play and the reality of the situation. The child can determine to role play a certain character or position and can just as easily determine to be herself again at any time in the play situation. In fantasizing, the child, and sometimes the adult, may lose touch with reality.

Children play out many things they do not understand through fantasy. Fantasies of family interactions are often observed in the housekeeping corner giving evidence of children trying to work through feelings and emotions which they do not understand. Boys and girls are seen spanking the baby or loving the baby. Listening to the conversation which accompanies the play often indicates that the actions betray wants, needs, or fears which children have. Just as children play to understand the cognitive and physical aspects of their environment, so also do they play to understand the emotional aspects.

We must understand that the children choose materials and activities which they can handle. Our culture imposes limits on children in that we provide certain play experiences and certain play materials for them to use. Thus, children growing up on the south side of Chicago will have a very different set of play opportunities and play materials than children growing up on a farm in Indiana. Although some aspects of urban and rural children's lives will be similar, there will be many differences. The opportunity for fantasy play may be very different also depending upon the opportunities available. However, even with these differences growth processes in children will direct their play and the use of whatever materials are available. For example, a preschool age girl in the city may play at imitating her mother who works in a factory. In her play, she might get a doll ready to go to the baby sitter like her mother gets her and her baby sister ready each day. She could pretend to stop by the delicatessen to pick up something for dinner. She could turn on the oven to warm the precooked dinner and play with the baby while waiting for their dinner to heat. A little preschooler from a midwestern farm might imitate her mother who stays at home all day. She pretends to bake, makes lunch to take to her husband in the field, gives the baby a bath and nap, and talks on the phone to a friend. Both children are imitating their mothers, but in very different ways based on their life experiences.

The Development of Roles and Actions in Fantasy Play

Children assume many roles in their play. They also assign roles to inanimate objects that they can manipulate. A doll or a toy, a piece of rope or a blanket, can become something dependent upon them. This can change children's status, in the sense that everything is now under their control; they are all-powerful and can induce these objects to do their bidding.

The child may also pretend to have an imaginary companion. The brighter the child the more likely to have a fantasy companion. This imaginary friend is very important and must be respected by parents and other family members. It is not at all unusual to observe this belief in a five or six year old. One five-year-old boy had an imaginary bear who lived in the basement. The bear never came upstairs but only played with the boy downstairs. He told other family members that the bear would not hurt them when they were downstairs because he was a friend.

There are also times when children assume the roles of animals or babies. The role of the baby is especially desirable when a child wants to enjoy something they believe they are too old for, that is, it allows them to indulge the desire to regress to an earlier age. By acting like a baby, they can enjoy activities or toys that younger children enjoy. I observed this behavior one day in a group of seven-year-olds who were second graders. They had been brought into a video taping laboratory to participate in a video taping session. When they walked in they saw some construction equipment usually found in kindergarten classrooms—parquetry blocks, plexiglass squares, rings and things—to be used in the taping session. They immediately began to play with the materials, obviously delighted to be doing so. But they spoke in high-pitched voices like younger children and even talked to each other about how they remembered playing with this equipment when they were "little."

Many of the roles children assume are those of adults or those involving social contacts. Usually there is a social quality which attempts to imitate some adult behavior, that is, it involves interaction and socializing behaviors. Children need this opportunity to imitate what is going on around them in order to understand the adult world. It reassures them as to the purpose and meaning of the adults' lives around them and allows for practice of the roles that they will later assume.

You need to provide props for play, such as dress up clothes, shoes, hats, purses, and belts to allow for more expression in the play. Children quickly use props for their play when the real thing is not around. Thus chairs, boards, blocks, and boxes can become a part of the play with little effort on the part of the children. The same props discussed in Chapters Three and Four can be used for fantasy play.

Often children who are undergoing stress or emotional tension will have to act out what they are feeling each day. An understanding parent or teacher can gently help the child through such a period. Helping the child verbalize feelings is important, too. Chapter Eight will guide you with children who need extra help at such times.

Imagination

The distinction between fantasy and imagination is difficult to determine. In this chapter we have treated fantasy as synonymous with day-dreaming or wishful thinking, and as the opposite of reality-oriented thinking, or real-life situations. The distinction we make between this and imagination is that imagination moves into the realm of creativity. This aspect leads to changes in the child or adult's life. It moves beyond a feeling of "If I could be . . ." or "I want to be . . ." to "What if I could be . . .". The mind tries many new ways of behaving and thinking, some of which are integrated into the real life world. Imagination in this sense is especially critical for modern adults. It will become even more so for the adult lives of the children with whom we are now working. Society is changing at such a rapid pace that it is impossible to comprehend what the adult lives of today's children will be like in 30 years. Thus, fostering imagination and creative behavior in children is a necessity for their survival and perhaps for that of society as a whole.

Childhood is an important time for the development of imagination. It is the time when one can more freely explore and develop the sense of curiosity upon which imagination feeds because the child is free to experiment. The child can play around with ideas and new perspectives and he can get a feel for and test out thoughts and ideas through imagination. With the young child this is difficult because young children have problems differentiating between fantasy and reality. As the child's reality base widens, imagination has a firmer foothold and the child has a basis for imaginative endeavors.

Children need the opportunity to pursue their imagination in many directions. Nursery school programs have traditionally provided for cognitive pursuits, such as arts, music, dances, and literature. Unfortunately, many kindergarten and primary school programs close off most of these endeavors in favor of academic programs that may or may not foster the more creative, cognitive pursuits. These pursuits need to be encouraged and provided for throughout the elementary grades and especially in the kindergarten-primary levels.

Each child begins early in life to develop idiosyncratic or personalized ways of coping with life tasks. Ways of coping may be revised with growth and plans may be altered. Former patterns may be replaced with new ones.

The child may develop a unique style of coping. These changes take place partly because of new experiences and partly because of the results of learning through fantasy and imaginative play.

Make-believe aids children in imitation. In imitation children attempt to act and talk like adults or other real persons. Much of this play reflects their attempt to be like familiar adults either in their immediate environment or on television. The element of nonreality, or make-believe, helps to make the attempt by broadening the world of play for children.

Imagination in Creative Endeavors

You can see imagination used in many ways by children. In a situation where art materials are available, we can watch them use color, texture, shapes, and space to create collages and other art forms. We can watch them working with paint, glue, glitter, paste, and rubber cement to hold materials together in some kind of creation representing their ideas. Children need freedom to work with these materials and to explore their ideas. Unless they have time and freedom to do what they wish, this aspect of imagination is hindered and kept from developing.

For children under five years of age you must keep in mind that creative art work does not usually begin with the finished product in mind. For this reason, it is a good idea not to give children patterns to copy or to show them a model to use for their work. The final product should evolve from their use of the material. It should represent the feelings and ideas they have as they work on projects. For this reason also, an art or creative media area should be available each day and children should be allowed to return to the same or a similar art experience as long as their interest remains.

Unlike many art experiences which seem to change daily for children, the woodworking bench usually has the same tools and the same materials available. Here again you see children developing their ideas and representing life as they understand it. Three pieces of wood nailed one on top of the other and painted blue can be a boat for a three- or four-year-old, a seven- or eight-year-old may add decks, masts, and sails. A five-year-old once decided to build a cat house for some kittens. He used plywood for room dividers in a cardboard box, cut a neat door in one end, and put old rags down for bedding. His "cat house" looked very much like a doll house from above. He could not understand why it did not appeal to the kittens who still wanted to curl up with their mother in a box. His concept of a house was applied to his creation, but this did not match the needs of the kittens to be near their mother. She and the kittens could not fit comfortably into the new house.

Work with clay, play dough, plasticene, and other maleable materials is especially suitable for developing imagination and encouraging creative effort. Children need to see how to roll and mold material with their hands. They should be able to enjoy the feel of the material and to shape it any way they please. They can be encouraged to poke it, or pinch it, press it out, pile it up or make holes in it. They sometimes enjoy working with it while they stand up and walk around the table. Variations can be used with sawdust dough and with shells, feathers, stones, wood, seeds, or other materials. Children are very proud of such products and adults need to show their appreciation of them and show respect for the child's ideas and creative results.

Other related activities are sand, mud, and water play. The sand box or sand table allows for all levels of imaginative endeavors. I observed a group of two through six-year-olds playing in an outdoor sand structure one summer. The very young children (just under three years of age) were sitting in the sand individually exploring the feel of it and ignoring one another. One was covering his leg completely with the sand and wiggling his toes just beyond the mound of sand. The other was filling an ice cube tray and dumping it out. Some four-year-olds were standing at the concrete structure in the middle of the sand structure building roads of sand on the concrete "table" and running small cars and trucks over the road. They were talking with one another about their play.

In a third group, five-year-olds were building sand tunnels together. Four boys were working cooperatively to build tunnels through which they placed their hands and some toy trucks. They were exploring the structure necessary for keeping the tunnels open and at the same time having fun discovering each other's fingers down in the tunnel. These different age groups represent the different levels at which children's imagination and exploration can operate with the same medium in the same area at the same time.

Music, movement, and dance lead to imaginative experiences for children. Closing one's eyes and thinking about music can lead to far away places or to feelings and emotions not experienced in everyday life. Scarves, hats, and flowing skirts can add a sense of another time, or another place. A child can become an elephant, a ballerina, or even the sugar plum fairy by listening to music. Dance and movement activities let children respond to the tempo or rhythm of the music. Many good ideas spring out of such sessions, and self-awareness and body awareness are enhanced.

Literature plays a key role in imagination. Exposure to ideas, characters, and experiences remote from children's lives all add power to the imagination. As children listen to stories or read their own, ideas lead to ideas. Words for expressing ideas and feelings can be obtained from the stories they hear. Chants and rhymes are repeated over and over again. The children's own stories emerge in their play and in their school work. Many times children choose to talk through puppets or to work their stories into puppet shows. Children's television shows have acquainted children with many kinds of puppets so many models are available to them.

It is difficult at times to separate the use of imagination, curiosity and creative endeavor from structured learning experiences. Perhaps they are too interwoven to even try. One such area that should be considered here is the interest children have in science and scientific endeavors. Insects, animals, and birds hold most children's interest. How things work, such as telephones, engines, and balancing apparatus, and what happens to objects when they are acted upon also intrigue children. Most good programs have a science component for all age levels. Also do not overlook the many opportunities children have at home to study insects, animals, and chemical and physical changes. You should provide many opportunities for children to develop their senses and sensory related feelings. Help children explore such things as mold on bread or an orange, changes in the weather, differences in rocks and earth structures, plants growing and changing, and even their own bodies changing.

By second and third grade many children are showing interest in specific areas of science. Their interest areas should be encouraged. Experiments encourage problem solving skills. Dewey talks about the need for observation skills.[2] Realizing that observation is an active process, he discusses how educators can encourage children to refine their skills. Observation involves delving into the unknown. Using the function of an object or the structure it possesses as a basis, you can help children to develop keen observation skills. Function and structure serve as focal points. Dewey also advocates that observation be scientific in nature, that is, children need to hypothesize and test their ideas. Facts need to be presented to stimulate the imagination so that possibilities that seem remote will be considered. Imagination can serve to sharpen observation skills.

Although television is often blamed for stifling children's imagination and creativity, it also brings many vivid experiences into their lives. Modern children are aware of many real life experiences that children of earlier periods in our history never chanced to see. Today's children understand much that is happening in the world around them, and if their parents discuss events with them, they are very likely to benefit from the exposure.

Imagination, then is a vital part of the development of a child. We have shown how it develops through play in many aspects of the child's life. Cognitive, psychomotor, and emotional growth are all intertwined in the child's everyday play.

Recreational Activities

Play gradually evolves into organized games and activities as the child approaches the elementary school years. Although spontaneous play activities still occur, more activities with rules are included in the child's play in contrast to the earlier years of life. Recreational pursuits involving other family members also develop. Although a child may be included in outings and various family activities at a very early age, the child becomes more involved and more of a contributor with age.

Games

Most of our discussion to this point has been concerned with how children come to master their environment through play. As the level of sophistication increases, interest in mastery of the games develops. Also, the child is better equipped to handle games. The change from spontaneous play activity characterized by fantasy to games characterized by rules is gradual. There is a fluctuation between the two depending upon how comfortable the children are with the rules of the game, the mix of children, their moods, external conditions, and a host of other factors. Sometimes, particularly in competitive games children cannot stand the thought of losing and will act against the rules. They may make up their own rules or disrupt the game completely, for instance messing up the cards in a card game or the players on the board of a checker game. Games can be classified in several ways. One way is to classify them by two large classes: individual games and social games. Individual games according to Stern have several categories of increasing complexity.[4] They include:

(1) mastery of the body where motor games use the body as an instrument
(2) mastery of things including both constructive and destructive games
(3) impersonation which includes transformation of people and things.

In social games, Stern includes pure imitation, games with more than one participant, and fighting games. Even with this distinction it is difficult to determine the real difference between individual and social games.

We are concerned in this section with those games, either individual or social which include rules. Practice play which was discussed in Chapter One relative to Piaget is an important lead-in to games with rules. In practice play the child has learned some of the limitations placed on him by others, by materials and equipment, and by individual physical or cognitive abilities. Added to these elements are rules of the game.

Games with rules are of two kinds. The first kind is organized rounds and singing games, such as Poor Sally, and Looby Loo, where children move around in a circle. This is followed by games like Farmer In The Dell, In and Out the Window, or London Bridge. As children learn to wait turns and follow directions, these kinds of games get more complex. Simple lotto or board games are the beginning of table games for two or more players. Children work through these games by the end of the primary grades. Old Maid, Animal Rummy, and other simple card games are also of interest to primary age children.

Games requiring skills with balls, ropes, running, and jumping take the form of relays and exercises at school. This is followed by team sports which may begin as early as third grade. Jump rope rhymes and chants might also be considered in this category since specific patterns must be followed or the child misses a turn or takes a turn holding the rope. Dodge ball and other group games are favorites of younger school age children. Hide and seek, tag, and King of the Mountain can all be played by second and third graders.

Concern has been expressed for those children who enter into competitive sports as early as seven or eight years of age. This is a period of rapid physiological and psychological growth. Since bone growth is more rapid than muscle growth at this time, there is a tendency for dislocation of joints and permanent injury to bones. Another important consideration is the child's emotional capacity to compete with others. Some children are pushed too soon into competitive sports by ambitious parents who want an athlete in the family. They cannot cope with the demands either psychologically or physiologically, and often their parents cannot either.

Another concern about organized sports is that time spent in them reduces the time the child has for free and spontaneous play. The need for time to develop through play continues through the primary grades. Parents and teachers should be sure that children have time for spontaneous, free play especially when their children are engaged in organized sports.

Organized sports can be a positive factor in the child's development at a later time. Learning to work as a team member, understanding the nature of competitive behavior, and accepting team discipline are all valuable learning experiences when offered at the appropriate time.

Other Recreational Activities

Young children can and should be included in family recreation, such as fishing, swimming, hiking or camping. The extent of this involvement should be regulated by safety considerations and the children's abilities to persevere. Children should always wear life jackets when they are in boats or canoes. If they are taken fishing along a bank of a river or a lake, they should be watched very carefully and perhaps should even wear a life jacket there. A three-year-old was on a dock with his father and a friend when he suddenly leaned over too far to see a minnow swimming by. He fell into four feet of water which was over his head. His father had to jump in and pull him out. When he returned home, he told his mother, "I almost swimmed. I went in the lake and almost swimmed." He had no idea of the danger his life was in.

Likewise, precautions should be taken on plans for hiking or camping with young children. Preschoolers can only walk so far. If a long hike is planned, either leave the young ones at home or plan to have someone carry them part way. Hiking and camping should always be planned with young children's snack times and nap times in mind. If children get too tired, it is often very difficult to get them to sleep and a good trip can be ruined.

Good planning will let even two-year-olds go persimmon hunting, mushroom hunting, or berry picking, but you must be watchful. Children try to pop toadstools in their mouths or pick up snakes. While the former activities may not be available in all parts of the country, many other substitutes can be found, such as shell hunting in the coastal regions.

Tension Release

Active play is a good outlet for tension. Behaviors, such as thumb sucking, nail biting, head banging, or hair pulling indicate tension and anxiety. Ilg and Ames believe that these are tension-relieving behaviors which serve as outlets for tensions which build up in the child.[2] Nagging the child to stop will not help. In fact when such behaviors occur, keeping a calm, relaxed attitude is best. Problems such as temper tantrums are often caused by frustration in the child. More space to move around in or activities to occupy the child may be the answer. Discovering the cause of the tantrums is a better solution than just handling them as they come. Large muscle exercise is often a good way for releasing tension. Make sure there is plenty of space to run and move about in, in the classroom as well as the home.

NOTES

1. Annie L. Butler, Edward Earl Gotts, and Nancy L. Quisenberry, *Early Childhood Programs: Developmental Objectives and Their Use,* (Columbus, Ohio: Charles E. Merrill Publishing Company, 1975), pp. 165–172.

2. John Dewey, *How We Think,* (Chicago: Henry Regnery Company, 1933).

3. Frances L. Ilg and Louise Bates Ames, *Child Behavior,* (New York: Dell Publishing Company, 1955).

4. W. Stern, *Psychology of Early Childhood,* (New York: Henry Holt and Co., 1924).

CHAPTER

SEVEN

Play items can be found in the kitchen—spoons and spatulas, empty food containers, tubes from waxed paper.

Materials
that Facilitate Play

One way to encourage children to play is through the careful choice of toys and play materials provided for them at home or in an educational program. In this chapter we are going to examine some of the criteria for selecting toys and play materials to facilitate play and some of the pitfalls to avoid if possible in the selection of materials. Very few of us have the kind of equipment budget required to buy all of the materials needed for a class of children, so we will offer some assistance to you by suggesting some creative ways for you to make use of discarded materials and some ways for you to create toys of your own.

Before we discuss criteria for selecting these materials, we would like to discuss our point of view about toys and their uses. Sometimes toys are labeled educational, which may be partially correct, but it is more accurate to say that play is educational and toys are but one factor in the educational value of play. The toys that children have available can either provide encouragement and stimulation to play or they can hamper children's inclination to play creatively.

Toys have been regarded as significant determinants for whether children play creatively or whether they play in a restricted or limited way. Several investigations have sought to determine the relationship between toys and the creativity of the child's play. Phillips [1] found that children who use less realistic toys create a larger number of themes in their play than children who use more realistic toys. A recent investigation by Pulaski [2] supported these findings; however, a similar study by McFarland [3] failed to show that toys which realistically imitate real objects produced fewer verbal uses than less realistic toys.

There is little doubt that adults feel more comfortable with nonstandard uses of less realistic toys than with nonstandard uses of realistic toys. If you are limited in the variety of materials which you can provide, it may be well worth your time to include a number of less realistic materials which you can encourage the children to use in nonrealistic ways.

Criteria for Selecting Equipment for Purchase

In this section we will examine the factors to be taken into consideration in the selection and purchase of toys and equipment. Some of these factors relate directly to the social and cultural interests of the community and school. Toys play a role in helping children to establish social and ethnic values that are important to their self-esteem, especially if the children are members of a minority group that may have a greater need to feel accepted and understood. In a classroom where there is a large number of Chicano children, you should not have all "white" dolls but you may not want to have all Chicano dolls either. You need to make available other objects common in the lives of the children from which they can create experiences common to them. If it should happen that you do not know what kind of toys the children play with at home and what experiences the children imitate in their play at home, you may want to consult with parents before making expensive purchases.

Recently, much attention has been called to the sexist nature of certain toys. This is apt to be an area about which many parents have very definite ideas, from a belief in the need for nonsexist materials to a feeling that certain materials should be used by only girls and certain toys by only boys. Most early childhood teachers need a much stronger awareness of the relationship of their own behavior to the behavior of children and of the sexist aspects of toys and toy usage before they can effectively guide children. You can, however, easily become aware of the different ways in which children are depicted in items such as puzzles, books, pictures, and packaging. You can also become aware of the different ways you treat boys and girls and become increasingly able to accept their behavior as people rather than as males or females. If you are behaving in a very stereotypical way, you may need to consider what constitutes equal treatment for all children.

Almost every community has individual differences affecting some of the equipment acquired for classrooms. Locally manufactured materials are more readily available and can be acquired more economically because no shipping costs are involved. Many parents may be employed in a specific industry, creating special local interest in that field. Some children may come from a cultural background that has colorful costumes, interesting games, and holidays different from those celebrated in the country as a whole. Another variation may result from the use of waste materials from local industries which can make good classroom materials. You need to be on your toes to discover these sources before they are overrun with teachers and children.

Many materials must be purchased and you must take certain criteria into consideration.

Interest. Will the toys interest the children? Interest is sometimes related to how attractive the play material is. Color, shape, size, and uniqueness can determine whether children are attracted to a toy initially. Whether interest continues is related to the variety of ways the child can use the toy and its suitability to the skills of individual children as well as their ability to use it to relate to their experience.

Observing the games children choose to play is one way for the teacher to determine the interest value of various materials. Children's conversation is another indicator. Perhaps most helpful to the teacher is knowledge of the developmental behavioral levels of the children used in conjunction with these observations.

Some of the most interesting materials are simple materials that can be used in a variety of ways by children of different abilities. The same materials interest children from the preschool through the primary years because of what they can do with them. If you give raw materials such as sand, water, clay, and paint to three-year-olds, you can expect a great deal of exploratory and manipulative action. One who has not observed three-year-olds might never believe their sustained interest in pouring water from one container to another or in using plain water to paint the wall or sidewalk. Probably every teacher has removed one dripping page painted solid with tempera paint only to have the child start a clean page which eventually ends up the same way. It is quite a transition from that to the primary child who has good control of the paint and uses it skillfully to conceptualize a recent trip to the circus. Throughout this age span paint is a high interest item. Interest is equally great for clay if children are provided with real potters clay that is just hard enough not to be sticky.

Adaptability. Will the material adapt to more than one purpose, more than one child or more than one age level? One of the real assets of such equipment as blocks and paint is that they can be used in more than one way by more than one child and by children of different ages. They can be used by the more product oriented six to eight-year-old child as well as the process-minded younger child.

Part of the test of adaptability is whether a toy suggests one particular use or many uses. For example, raw materials such as sand can be used by a child to pour from one pail to another, to make a simple tunnel or to provide food in the playhouse. With an older child it can be used to make an elaborate sand castle or as an ingredient in a permanent concrete structure. Clay can be rolled into balls and snakes or it can be used to make beautiful pottery. Various wheel toys that can be ridden also have great adaptability. Although younger children need to focus on the skill of riding a tricycle, slightly older children use it for a horse, fire engine or automobile. Older children test their skill riding bicycles without hands and in treacherous places. Belonging to the group is dependent upon developing the skill of bike riding to a high level. This ability is required to participate in games that utilize the greater mobility that has been acquired by the eight-or nine-year-old.

Schools find that adaptable toys are essential because of the range of interests and abilities in a group of children and the requirement that toys be used over a period of time in order to justify their cost and maintenance.

Safety. Does the material comply with safety standards? Construction should be carefully examined. Is the material unbreakable? Is it painted with non-poisonous paint? Is it free from sharp edges and detachable parts that can lodge in a windpipe, ear or nose? Is it easily cleaned? Is it free from parts that can pinch fingers or toes or catch hair?

In discussing toy safety it is essential to distinguish between the characteristics of the toy itself and the use of the toy. Characteristics of the toy refers to construction and production. A toy that breaks with normal usage is not very safe. Every year children are poisoned from eating the paint on their cribs and toys. An otherwise acceptable truck may have sharp pointed fenders or bumpers. Stuffed animals that cannot be washed harbor germs which may be transmitted to the users. Electric toys are unsafe for young children; they do not yet understand how to handle them safely.

Children under proper supervision may be permitted to use some toys and materials which could be potentially dangerous. A good example is the school use of hammers, saws, nails and woodworking materials. The key to safe usage lies in supervision. Such materials should not be available to children at times when they cannot be adequately supervised. Usually, their use must be confined to a specified area. It is important to limit the number of children working with tools to the number who can work safely in the space available. Other examples of the proper use of potentially dangerous materials are: the use of kitchen utensils, such as paring knives, in the preparation of fruit or vegetables to be eaten by the children, the use of a hot plate for cooking experiences that provide many learning opportunities as well as much enjoyment.

Despite many parents' feelings about violence and the use of weapons, most children have some kind of toy gun or pistol at one time or another and these weapons are sometimes brought to school. Teachers in individual schools handle this situation in different ways. Some are so opposed to the use of guns that toy guns are put away from the time they arrive at school until they go home. Other teachers permit limited usage on the playground where danger is minimal. Toy guns and other weapons are not usually considered appropriate school equipment because they present real safety hazards when pointed directly at someone's face. Children have great difficulty remembering not to get too close to other children with a toy gun so most teachers forbid their use as a safety precaution.

Sturdiness. Is the material sturdy enough to withstand the use a child will make of it? Nothing is more frustrating than a toy which breaks while still new and nothing is a greater waste of money than such a toy. A safe prediction is that some misuse of toys will occur in every classroom. Examining loose or weak parts and avoiding toys with breakable springs or batteries that wear out is usually wise with younger children. Anything big enough to be sat upon must be sturdy enough to hold children. They will ride surprisingly small vehicles, climb into doll carriages, sleep on doll beds, and ride on wagons that were never intended to hold the weight of a child.

The constant and continued use of school equipment makes durability a prime requisite. Good equipment may cost more initially, but it is worth the cost if it lasts longer and needs fewer repairs. For schools, the most sturdy and durable materials available are usually recommended both to avoid high replacement and repair costs and to avoid accidents. Since some equipment may be permanently installed outdoors, the ability to withstand harsh weather conditions may be a factor. Any equipment which does not have some measure of protection must have unusual strength and durability to withstand weather and use hazards. When older children have access to the equipment for younger children, strength can be a particularly important factor.

Encouragement of Large and Small Muscle Development. Does the toy encourage the development of large and small muscle coordination? Because young children are growing rapidly and need to do things which will assist in the development of large muscles essential to coordination and movement, they need equipment which will encourage them to climb, lift, ride wheel toys, push, pull and tug, and balance. For children in primary grades, equipment is still vitally important to maintain proper physical fitness and to develop the skills which enable them to compete physically with other children. At this point children begin to take interest in team sports, such as basketball, baseball, softball and football and use real equipment rather than toys. They are also interested in learning to ice skate and roller skate. Schools should continue to provide materials for large muscle activity, but if playground equipment is lacking, children of this age enjoy jumping rope, playing hopscotch, and playing group games involving large muscle activity, such as follow-the-leader or dodge ball.

It is also important to have activities which aid in the development of small muscles and in eye-hand coordination. For the very young child, this small muscle activity may be stacking small blocks or putting rings on the color cone. Gradually, the toys should demand the finer coordination required by beads, peg boards, puzzles, and construction toys, such as tinker toys and small plastic shapes that fit together. Later, children develop finer coordination by constructing Lincoln Logs and building with Erector sets. These toys can be used to create elaborate designs, or a house furnished with chairs, beds, and tables cut and folded by the children. Art materials, such as crayons, paint, fingerpaint and clay are adaptable to wide ranges of small muscle development provided the child chooses how to use them. Manipulative skills that children learn in playing with materials, such as pencils, crayons and chalk, which require fine muscle coordination are helpful in acquiring the control necessary for writing. Even after they have acquired a high degree of small muscle control, children still need materials which help to perfect eye-hand coordination. For example, a child may need to sew a puppet's clothing or construct a bird or doll house, which requires adult help in supplying necessary materials.

Strengthen Social Relationships with Other People. Does the material provide for social activity? Children need materials which encourage both independent and social activity. Materials, such as blocks, housekeeping furniture and accessories, climbing apparatus, and dress-up clothes encourage children to do things together. These materials require that they do things cooperatively, and that they interact with other children as they assume different roles. They are able to learn much about other children's responses and to understand some of the perplexing bits of information which have come to them through their daily experiences. Much of the value of dramatic play and sociodramatic play, as discussed in Chapter Four, cannot happen unless children have materials that encourage their acting out.

In a primary classroom, where it may not be so easy to provide activities for strengthening social relationships, it may be possible to encourage some socializing through the use of games requiring two or more children to interact. A costume collection may encourage creative dramatics and bring about much interaction as children select roles and make decisions about what the characters will do.

Build Competencies for Living in the World. Will the materials build a variety of understandings at the child's level? Some materials need to be selected to stimulate cognitive development and academic skills. Books can be used with children. They can get interested in looking at the pictures or pointing to something and having an adult or older child name what it is.

If teachers are careful in the selection of books for young children, they can gradually build, not only the children's vocabularies and their informational backgrounds, but they can also create a desire to read. Books for preprimary children should be about things they encounter in their environment, objects, animals, and people. Some of these early books will have more pictures than stories and do not have to have continuity from one page to the next. The teacher can use the pictures as a basis for talking with the child. Two-year-old children will listen to the shortest, simplest story if the adult uses a lot of interest holding techniques, such as letting the child participate in telling the story by naming a character, incorporating the child's name into the story, and creating a feeling of suspense by the way the teacher moves from one page or action to another.

During the preschool years between three and six, a wide selection of simple stories, well illustrated with attractive pictures is available. Schools should try to buy children's books in library bindings because these last longest and will withstand usage. Many of the same books that can be read to preschool children will be the books children read to themselves during the six- to eight-year-old period. Public library collections of children's books are available to both families and schools and usually the children's librarian is helpful in finding the right book for the child. Hopefully, the school will have its own library from which children can check out their own books.

Many of the materials in the science area, such as magnifying glasses, magnets, buzzers, aquaria, and terraria contribute to children's cognitive development. In the area of math there are games which involve counting, puzzles which assist in learning one-to-one correspondence, scales which encourage weighing, and cash registers which encourage learning about money. Measures of volume and distance can be learned in connection with many everyday activities. Bingo games are excellent for teaching matching; small blocks and beads which come in different colors, sizes and shapes can be used for both matching and classification. If commercial materials are not available, collections of buttons, leaves, stones and other materials can be used.

For teachers who want to encourage play with numerals and letters, large wooden or plastic letters and numerals are available to spell out children's names and to represent the number of objects available. Flannel board numerals and letters are also available for children who have greater motor coordination. They may want to leave out what they have made to show to other people. If the teacher is careful to follow the child's lead in using letters and numerals, the child can learn and have fun, too. If the teacher pushes, the materials may be abandoned. Primary children enjoy using letters to make words, and finding the letters is easier than writing them. They also like to have words spelled out that can be used in composing stories, and they enjoy games which require counting and reading directions.

Arouse Imagination and Creative Thinking. Will use of the material stimulate imaginative and creative ideas? Instead of doing everything for the child, materials, such as paint, fingerpaint, clay, sand, and water encourage the expression of feelings and encourage children to use their imaginations. For this to happen, the materials must be provided in sufficient quantities to encourage freedom of use, and the teacher's guidance must be facilitating and encouraging rather than restricting and adult-initiated or directed.

Other kinds of materials, such as those used to imitate housekeeping or to enact the roles of adults in the children's environment, can be helpful in the expression of ideas. Sometimes a cash register added to the block area or a telephone added to the housekeeping area gives new direction to the play and stimulates new ideas. A blanket over a card table creates a hideaway and may provide the background for enactment of many kinds of play. Knowing the experiences a child has had can help in suggesting the kind of materials useful for the expression of ideas.

Older children have more opportunity to be creative because their ability to sustain interest for more than one day, and some of their materials, enable them to build semi-permanent structures which can be used for several days. If they have the opportunity to use more than one medium in their creations, and if they are aided by tape recorders for storytelling so their imaginations are not limited to their writing abilities, their imagination and creativity can be greatly enhanced.

Assisting Parents in Selecting Toys

In general, the same criteria apply to the selection of materials for children to use at home that apply to the selection of toys for school use. You want to help parents think about their children's interests. Most families cannot afford to purchase toys that their children will not be interested in. Neither can many parents afford to provide the variety of toys that should be available in a good nursery school or kindergarten. Parents are in a good position to make decisions about toys for individual children because they have much more opportunity to observe what their children play with when left to their own resources.

You may want to help a family with several children find materials that children of several ages can enjoy. You might help them start with a small set of blocks that can be added to, to make more elaborate constructions as the children get older. You might need to interpret that it is all right to buy a boy a doll or to buy a girl a truck or train, because parents, especially fathers, sometimes want their children to choose stereotypical masculine or feminine toys before it matters to the children.

Most parents buy a few, small, inexpensive toys from time to time which are not expected to last very long and which their children enjoy very much. Small plastic cars and trucks, tiny dolls, small plastic tea sets, toy animals, and card games, are often prized by children but would not be purchased for a school because they would be quickly lost or broken. Sometimes you can help parents purchase such toys if they think they are worth the money and will last as long as the child will be interested in them. You still need to help parents avoid having a box of toys which will not work because this is just as frustrating at home as it is at school. The following section will deal with some of the pitfalls which parents and teachers frequently encounter in the selection of toys.

Pitfalls in the Selection of Materials

Sometimes we seem to forget that play is spontaneous and that the materials provided should be those which will be inviting to the child. We either consciously or unconsciously permit our needs to take precedence over the children's interests and fun. Knowing some of the common pitfalls may help you to avoid them.

Buying Toys Too Advanced for Children. We all know at least one father who bought his son an elaborate electric train set when a wooden push train would have been more appropriate. The young child cannot yet use electrical equipment safely nor can he or his friends manage to keep from stepping on the track or short circuiting the connections. Such a purchase is disappointing to both the child and the parent.

Another common, inappropriate purchase for preschool children is a doll that walks, talks, or requires careful treatment. The preschooler will cry for the doll and hold it to simulate walking. The former, inappropriate toy usually leads to frustration, because parents want the doll kept nice and the child has other ideas for its use. Assuming that most toys will stay nice is an almost equally common error.

At one time or another, we have all been guilty of buying books that are too difficult for a child at the time of purchase. At school we sometimes make the mistake of selecting books that are too long or do not offer enough action to hold children's attention. Fortunately, at school you can take the book back to the library or swap with another teacher whose children will enjoy the book. At home it is more difficult to correct the error particularly if we have fond memories of the book. What the parents probably do not remember is how old they were when they had the book. We can have a hard time dealing with our feelings if we are disappointed that the child has not been able to share what had delighted us as a child.

With primary children we sometimes have to be careful about two problems with books. If we buy books that are too difficult, children become discouraged and consequently may never go back at a later time when they could be read more easily. We may also give children books that they can read but cannot understand. Lack of understanding soon dulls interest in the book.

Buying What We Did Not Have as Children. All of us at one time or another have heard adults say, "If I ever have children, they are going to have . . . which I always wanted but didn't have as a child." The pitfall here is one of not understanding the point of view of the child. Most likely, many children have things they desperately want that parents for one reason or another do not think is the best thing for them to have at a particular time. Parents, of course, know of these wants but may not be aware of how desperately the item is wanted. Even if they do, the reason for not getting it may be a valid one. Maybe they are concerned for the child's safety; maybe they do not feel the purchase is worth the money; maybe they do not have the money; maybe they think that the child has other toys which are reasonably good substitutes. All reasons like these are difficult for young children to understand. Misunderstanding our parent's decision and feeling strongly about our wants, we later resolve that our children will not have to do without something they badly want. Parents may bend over backwards and get things a child does not really need and sometimes buy things that the child does not really want. This is also the kind of reasoning which sometimes underlies the purchase of too many toys at one time.

Too Many Toys at Once. Young children are easily overwhelmed by too many toys at once. They have difficulty making choices at any time and having so much at once can result in the child's being unable to choose a toy and stick with it for any appreciable length of time. Buying too many toys at once usually happens at Christmas and birthdays when parents and grandparents all give toys to children. Wise parents, who know grandparents are going to give a child toys for a special occasion, find other ways to do something special for the child, such as a trip to the beach, tickets to the theater, or picking out items of clothing with the child, such as a new purse, a wooly cap, or a new swim suit. When the child does get too much at one time, adults can put away some things which seem less attractive at the moment or which may be too advanced for the child. These do not really need to be hidden from the child, simply put away until the child asks for them or until the child is looking for something new or different to do.

A part of the same problem is having too many toys available at once. Young children are confused by everything piled in a toy box or crammed into a shelf. The result is that they pull everything out to find the one thing they want and the remaining toys are left to be walked over or swept aside, and eventually put away under strong protest. It is more desirable to select some of the toys that are not being used regularly and put them in a different place until they are wanted. Some games with small parts need to be put away where they cannot be spilled when not in use. It may be well, however, to let the children help with selecting things to put away and things to keep out, at least as a trial measure to see which ones they consider most important. Children, like adults, sometimes prize old and scarred toys and odd bits of things that adults label as junk. Even very young children often have strong preferences that need to be honored.

All classrooms should have more materials available than are actually out, and materials should be rotated from time to time. If a new order of toys arrives, some may be given to the children to use and others should be saved until something new is needed to pep up the program a bit. It always helps to have something new when there has been a long week of bad weather preventing the children from going outside.

Too Many Toys with Too Few Uses. In a previous section we referred to adaptability as one of the criteria for selecting materials. One question that we should ask in buying toys for children is "How many ways can the child use this?"

Materials such as blocks, dolls, paint, sand, and wheel toys come out very high on this list, but single purpose toys, such as puzzles and beads come out relatively low. This does not mean that puzzles should not be bought, only that the bulk of the money to be spent for toys should not be spent for puzzles. If one investment has been a set of floor blocks adequate for two or three children to play with, this can greatly enhance the value of such things as trucks, cars, small wooden animals, or small plastic or wooden people. The combination of activities the child can engage in has been greatly increased. The same is true if the child has a doll and a doll bed. The addition of such items as a doll carriage, an iron and ironing board, a tea set, or a telephone allows the child to elaborate upon the already familiar play theme of housekeeping, and the use is not limited to that immediately suggested by the item.

Buying Inferior Toys. We cannot rely on cost alone as a determining factor in whether a toy is a wise purchase. Quality related to the sturdiness and finish should never be ignored. Yet, not all stores carry a line of quality toys. Consequently, many toys must be ordered from catalogs without the opportunity to inspect them before purchase. In cities, a few department stores and gift shops usually carry high quality toys but such stores have difficulty keeping the really nice things in stock. Do not give up until you find a place that has nice toys. It is better to have one toy that lasts than two that are quickly broken. You also encourage children to take care of toys if the toy takes reasonable use without breaking. Toys that break without reason help the child think of the materials as expendable and apt to break.

You should try to avoid buying toys that have been made to look too "cute." Some toy makers have an exaggerated view that distorted faces, over-decorated wagons, comical animals and many other kinds of grossly exaggerated designs appeal to children. They don't. They sometimes do appeal to the adults who buy the toys for children. In general, the exaggerated design just makes the toy somewhat confusing to the child and possibly detracts from the variety of ways it may be used.

Another thing to avoid is a toy with too many gadgets that push in, pull out, wind up, or are loose, yet are required to make the toy do whatever it is supposed to do. Toys that do everything for the child at a touch of a button or turn of a key sometimes amuse a child, but usually they do not stimulate imagination or creativity. Usually, if the winding mechanism breaks or the batteries burn out, interest in the toy is quickly lost.

Too Many Toys That Are Supposed to Teach. Because we are so anxious for children to learn, we sometimes go overboard for "educational" toys. Usually, for preschool children, these are toys which are supposed to have a positive effect on success at school. For school age children such toys teach number combinations, spelling, reading or geography. The pitfall you want to avoid is over-emphasis on learning. Children enjoy having a few of the teaching kind of toys. They often enjoy even more having you play the game with them. This is also a point to consider. Many of these games cannot be played by children without you to interpret the rules, read the directions, or referee the disputes between children. There is a danger that this kind of play will lose not only some of its fun but also some of its spontaneity. We can give children a rather distorted view of play if we use it to manipulate them toward an academic goal.

Succumbing to Television Ads. Television ads for toys which appear on programs for children are very powerful in their influence on children's wants. When children are told repeatedly that they should get mother to buy a specific toy they are almost certain to respond. The problem for us is to distinguish between real wants and the kind of brainwashed wants that arise because of exposure to ads. Most of us have bought something that a child insisted upon having only to find out that once purchased the toy was soon forgotten. Perhaps one of the most sensible approaches to this problem lies in avoiding overexposure to television which occurs in many families.

We need to use the same criteria for evaluating toys advertised on television as for evaluating any toy. If they do not give a strong indication of holding children's interest or of being appropriate, then perhaps it would be better to purchase a more promising toy after determining its appeal.

Creating and Finding Playthings

Even if teachers have a good supply of materials they always need more. Many teachers, however, really do not have an adequate supply of materials to conduct a good program. If you are either handicapped by not having enough materials, or if you want more than you have, there are gold mines of discarded or waste materials which can be used to make your classroom more stimulating. You cannot afford to ignore the many practical and creative materials that can be obtained at little or no cost, and that with your ingenuity and that of your children can be interestingly used.

Solicit the assistance of your children and their parents. Almost every family has a few things around that they have discovered creative uses for that they will be glad to share. Children, particularly primary children, can learn to be alert to materials they can use in the classroom. Since children like to bring things to school, you can capitalize on this by sending a list of things you can use home with the children. This is a beginning. Another resource is your friends, even if they do little more than save frozen pie tins, plastic meat containers and plastic forks and spoons. Most of us have favorite stores where we shop and where the merchants or salespeople know us. By making a few inquiries you may discover that some of their throwaways can be useful to you and your children. Garage sales also offer some loot you can acquire for little expense. You need to learn to be a good scavenger, not only because you can find materials that will enrich your program but also because the children will follow your lead. Your attitude of finding varied uses for materials will be "caught" by your children, and when they catch on all kinds of unusual projects will begin to develop.

Sources of Free and Inexpensive Manufactured Materials. *Homes.* The list of materials that can be brought from homes is endless. Parents will probably need a little encouragement before they give you some of the items, so you will have to put the larger items, such as a crib mattress on your list as well as the bottles and cans that they will think of themselves.

Many of the most common items come from the kitchen—kitchen utensils, such as, spoons and spatulas, empty food containers, egg cartons, tubes from waxed paper and foil, aluminum pie plates, frozen dinner containers and other foil containers, baby food jars, frozen juice containers, milk and cream cartons of different sizes, strainers that are a little bent and don't quite come clean, discolored or chipped enamel saucepans, large glass jars to be used as terraria, jars with shaker tops, such as those that hold garlic salt or spices, plastic detergent bottles, bleach bottles and large cans which can serve as sand scoops or buckets. Also from the kitchen can come broken appliances like toasters, clocks, can openers, and broilers which could be used in a "fix-it" shop for the children to take apart. We so often tell children to take care of things that they can get real satisfaction from being permitted to legitimately take things apart.

The home is a prime source for materials for dramatic play. In asking for materials such as items of clothing for dress-up, be sure to ask for things for boys, too. Dress-up clothes will fit a little better and drag the floor less if some of them are clothes for larger boys and girls rather than adult clothes. It is nice if the clothes are washable, but sometimes this quality must be compromised, especially if attractive party clothes are contributed. Shoes, hats, costume jewelry, neckties, and scarves all are very useful. These items can be replaced at intervals providing new life for the housekeeping area; but do be careful about removing some child's favorite item without consent. Since it is very easy to acquire women's items, special care should be given to finding hats, boots, billfolds and other men's items.

Some of the larger items that homes might supply are pieces of ladders that are no longer totally useful, garden hoses, large metal or plastic tubs, buckets, pans, and large paint brushes no longer good enough for painting. The sewing center also yields varied materials—spools, scraps of cloth, scraps of lace, tape and other trimmings, and yarn.

If you can give parents a list with an assortment of items on it, they will be able to add some items you did not think to include. The important point is to make them conscious of what you can use.

Lumberyard or Cabinet Shop. It is almost never necessary to buy lumber for the workbench at full cost. Some cabinet shops will gladly permit you to take the scraps of wood out of their waste can for no charge at all or for a very minimum cost. Soft pieces of wood have to be selected for nailing and sawing, but small pieces of hardwood can be glued to make imaginative shapes. Lumberyards will also give you their scraps if you load them into your car yourself, and a lumber mill will probably give you any amount of sawdust you want which you can use like sand or put in "sawdust" clay. Asking them a few questions about when their scraps are emptied may provide a clue to the best time for making your trip to collect this material.

Stores. All stores that receive their stock packed in cardboard cartons have a supply of these cartons at one time or another. For large cartons which can be made into post offices, stores, and puppet theaters the furniture store is probably the best source although some department store items also are packed in large cartons. Another place to explore is a large appliance store where you might find boxes which have held stoves, washers, and refrigerators. These are large and sturdy enough to make a semi-permanent structure that can be retained in the classroom for a long time. These structures can be made more permanent with a water base latex paint, or if younger children want to do the painting, tempera paint can be used and later sprayed with shellac.

Just how far you go with the use of cardboard boxes may depend on how well equipped your classroom actually is. If you have easels, stoves, refrigerators, or even blocks, you will probably confine your use of cardboard to structures like grocery stores, garages, and houses that are only expected to last for a week or two. If you do not have larger items of furniture, they can be made from large, heavy cardboard boxes. A table easel can be made by taking a box which has either a bottom or sides large enough to hold the easel paper. Cut a triangular piece from the box so that the open side of the triangle serves as the base of the easel with one side holding the paper and the other side elevating the paper. Make holes at the top in which to insert clothes pins to hold the paper. Children will then be able to change their own easel paper. A flannel board may be made in the same way so that it will not tip over, or a straight piece of cardboard may be used that will lean against a chair.

Equipment for a housekeeping area is so expensive that many programs cannot afford all they would like to have. While not completely satisfactory, you can make a stove from a box about 18" x 18" x 27" in size. Stand the box on end, seal it except for one end flap which can be trimmed to make the back of the stove where the controls will be placed. Use another piece of cardboard to seal the back and brace this piece of cardboard. Paint the entire box the desired color with latex paint, then take black paint and paint burners on the top. Fasten some bottle tops to the extended piece in the back to make some controls. These also can be painted black before attaching. The main disadvantage to this stove is that it doesn't have an oven but this bothers adults more than children. Such a stove will last for quite a long time. The variety of furniture you can construct is limited only by the variety of boxes you can find and your time and imagination. If you can find enough sturdy boxes of the same size you can stuff them tightly with newspaper and use them for blocks. Any equipment you make will look better if you add a coat of latex paint, as well as being slightly reinforced by the paint. For a really big paint job on nursery school and kindergarten equipment, you can acquire the assistance of parents or of older school children. Primary children will be interested in painting their own equipment and can do a reasonably good job. Their satisfaction with the job is worth a few drips and smears. Once they have painted it, it is truly theirs.

The large ice cream carton is another very useful kind of container. A most obvious use for the large three gallon containers is as a waste basket. These cartons can be painted to match the decor of the room or covered with contact paper to give them a more durable surface. If a large enough space can be cut out of the side for the child's face they can be turned upside down and used as space helmets or divers' masks. These cartons are also good for storing bulky items which do not fit readily into the usual containers.

Many stores sell products with designs that change from one year to the next. Carpet stores, for example, will give you samples of discontinued designs and colors that can be used for individual mats to sit on in an uncarpeted classroom, for a carpet in a house made from a cardboard box, or for a throw rug in the housekeeping area. Tile stores will give away broken or cracked samples of vinyl flooring which can be cut into smaller shapes for matching or design making. Chipped ceramic tiles can be decorated to conceal the crack or chip. Wallpaper stores give away old wallpaper sample books which can be used in cutting, pasting, and painting. Fabric shops have pattern books and the cardboards and tubes that fabrics are wound on. Newspapers and print shops have many weights and colors of waste paper that can be used by children. We are sure you will be able to think of other stores in your neighborhood that are not listed here. Pay them a visit.

Other Manufactured Items.   A publication entitled *Playgrounds for Free,* Hogan,[4] describes the use of used and surplus materials in playground construction. This book not only identifies the materials but describes and illustrates how to make adventure playgrounds, people's parks, and how to obtain double duty from parking lots. Some of the materials which can be obtained free, or nearly so, are cable reels, tanks and drums, concrete pipe, utility poles, railroad ties, tires of all sizes, and inner tubes. This is in addition to such items as old trucks, cars, boats, railroad cars, and many other large throwaways.

Natural Materials. If the playground has no other suitable climbing apparatus, one potential source is part of a large tree that has been recently felled. Assistance of a number of parents and/or teachers will be needed to make a tree useable. Sections must be cut that are suitable for climbing, edges smoothed, and bark stripped from the trunk. Parts of it may have to be sunk into the earth to provide a steady base for climbing, and to prevent it from tipping or shifting position if too many children get on one side.

Sometimes it takes something as barren as a totally blacktopped playground built on a city roof to help you realize just how richly nature's materials can contribute to the classroom. Some of the most obvious natural materials are acorns, pinecones, sweetgum balls, leaves, seeds, seed pods, birds' nests, insects, frogs, tadpoles, turtles, stones, flowers, shells, snow, and sand. Some of these supply the basis for a science lesson, some can be combined with woodworking to make interesting three dimensional collages and objects, some provide the basis for interesting and attractive artistic productions. If you live near a woods or stream, or if your school is located in such an area, the possibilities for classroom materials change from season to season and never fail to capture the children's interest.

One of the nicest aspects of natural materials is their abundance at no cost. If you do not have an ample supply yourself, all you have to do is let parents and friends know that you want them. Children will bring them not just one day but more days than you probably want them to. They will also find many more uses than you would think of yourself if you foster the kind of atmosphere that encourages trying things out and using materials in different, nonrealistic ways.

Modification of Criteria for "Found" Materials. Two of the criteria identified earlier for consideration in the purchase of materials still hold true in the selection of "found" objects. These criteria are interest and safety. Many "found" objects have more interest appeal to children than manufactured materials. Very little in the way of commercial materials can compete with a frog, insect, or just water to hold the interest of children. If children are lacking in interest in "found" materials, you have no obligation to use them. The children might get real satisfaction out of finding a way to return them to nature.

Safety is an important consideration in many ways. If playground equipment is constructed of items you have located for no cost, you still must do whatever is necessary to make the playground as safe as any other playground. If you are gathering seeds, flowers, and pods, you need to know which plants are poisonous and how to help children identify the poisonous plants and leave them out of their collections. If you are collecting insects, you must know which ones to let the children handle and which ones should be left alone. Some very interesting ways to teach safety are presented in realistic situations which can be integrated into the curriculum.

Sturdiness is a criterion that has to be evaluated in terms of the total situation. Where sturdiness is related to safety, safety should be maintained. Sturdiness, however, is not always the most important consideration. If you choose between having a cardboard sink and stove or no sink and stove at all, it makes sense to choose the cardboard. Children can derive many hours of satisfying activity from it before it has to be replaced. A cardboard playhouse can be just as much fun to decorate as a wooden one, and when children tire of it, it can be forgotten. A storefront or a puppet stage made from cardboard serves its purpose quite well without requiring permanent storage when not in use.

In using "found" materials, your attitude toward adaptability can also be different. If little time or money is invested in the material, adaptability becomes less important than it might otherwise be. If the material serves a useful function, we do not have to concern ourselves with just how many purposes it serves. Fortunately, such materials as water, boxes, leaves, seed and many found materials are very adaptable.

Often it is possible to create objects or toys with a class, especially when the children get older and have ideas about how they want their equipment made. They happily engage in papier maché construction, design sculptures from boxes, and construct garages from cardboard. These constructions may be prized much more because of the enjoyment of doing and the sense of accomplishment they afford, than for the beauty or quality of the finished product. Evaluation of the activity must be on the doing and the creating rather than on the product.

Storage. Every classroom needs a variety of storage areas. Every classroom needs some kind of walk-in storage either adjoining the classroom or accessible to several classrooms. This space should have wide shelving to hold the larger equipment, and walls on which some things, such as ladders, can be hung and close to which bikes and wagons can be parked.

The shelves should be organized so that similar materials are placed together. Once the arrangement is complete, they should be labeled in order that material which is removed can be returned to the same shelf when not in use in the classroom. Small objects should be put in labeled boxes which are stackable and neat. This keeps the storage area neat even though its contents are the kind that frequently lead to a cluttered appearance.

You should have some classroom storage which is high and accessible only to the teacher. This is a good place to keep games that are not for children to use at their discretion. These games may be available to the children upon request or they may be taken out by the teacher when needed. Games that require special supervision or have small parts that are easily lost fall into this category. You may also find this a convenient place to store puzzles not in immediate use or musical instruments which need to be readily available but should not be placed on open shelves or hung on a pegboard. Other items which may be placed high in closed cabinets are first aid supplies, sewing supplies, extra clothing, paper towels, tissues, and toilet tissue.

Most of the storage used by the children should be open shelving. Open shelving enables them to see materials that are available and encourages them to use them. They cannot see materials kept behind closed cabinet doors. Materials which are placed on open shelves should have a place where they are regularly kept enabling the children to find a toy and put it back. Toys also should not be cluttered, rather they should be arranged in an orderly fashion on the shelves. This means that enough storage should be provided in the different interest areas of the room to hold the materials used there rather than trying to crowd everything into one or two shelf sets in the same part of the room.

Creating Your Own Materials. Even in schools that have an adequate budget for materials and equipment, you will find there are times when you need to create some games and activities that children enjoy. Some of these games and other creations will be relatively permanent and you will want to finish them as nicely as possible. Even if they are made of cardboard you will want to laminate them so they will withstand ordinary use. Other creations will be for one-time use and then thrown away. Having materials of your own creation is one way to keep from ever finding yourself in a classroom with no manipulative materials.

If you plan to create play materials, the suggestions below may be helpful.

1. Be a saver. Learn to tell when something about to be thrown away may have a future use, for example, magazines with many pictures, old workbooks, old books in which the binding has come apart, large posters or pictures at least 8½ by 11 inches, and all kinds of cardboard and boxes.
2. Acquire a kit of basic tools. You need large scissors, a utility knife, a good hammer, nails, a jigsaw, glue, ruler, felt-tip markers, paper, cardboard, and paint.
3. Buy materials seasonally when you can get them for less, or watch for sales. Some items, such as tape, paint, glue, foil, paper or plastic cups, and contact paper are sometimes advertised by discount stores at very low prices.
4. Organize and store materials so you can tell what you have and so you can find them easily. Junk does not have to look junky.
5. If possible, keep your materials near the place where you do your work.

The following are some examples of games and toys you can make.

1. Wooden puzzles. Paint a picture on a piece of thin plywood approximately 10 by 12 inches. Draw off puzzle pieces and use a jigsaw to cut out pieces.

2. Lotto Games. Make a card with 6 to 12 pictures on it. Then make small cards with one picture identical to those on the larger card. These can be pictures of objects, animals, fruits, birds, or flowers. Sometimes an old workbook with colored pictures is a good source for these pictures.

3. Sequence Cards. Cut out the pictures in a comic strip. Laminate each one on a separate piece of cardboard and have the children put them together in sequential order.

4. Rhyming Puzzles. Put rhyming words and pictures on tagboard. Laminate. Cut apart with an irregular pattern to make a puzzle. Cut each card in a different way so the cards can only be matched correctly.

5. Sandpaper Letters. Cut letters from sandpaper or form them with yarn and glue on cardboard squares.

6. Puppets. Make sock, finger, or paper bag puppets. Paint on faces to make animals or storybook characters. Puppets for one-time use can be made from potatoes.

7. Feel Box. Take a fairly large box or ice cream carton with a removable top that will hold a child's hand and one or more objects. Cut a hole in the side large enough for a child's hand to go through and attach the top of a sock to it for the child to put his hand through. Put objects in through the top of the box.

8. Alphabet Puzzles. Put an uppercase letter on the left half of a cardboard and the same lowercase letter on the right half of the same cardboard. Cut the cardboard apart so pieces will not fit together if they are not the same letter.

9. Designs. Paint designs using different colors or shapes on cardboard that can be copied with beads, small blocks, or tangrams. Ask the children to use the materials to construct the designs.

10. Sandpaper Blocks. Glue or nail sandpaper to small wooden blocks.

11. Shakers. Fill dried gourds, small metal boxes, salt boxes with beans, rice, or bells and close opening. Use the same container with different materials inside to observe differences in the sounds made by the materials.

12. Clonkers. Save two halves of a coconut shell and hit them together.

13. Sound Glasses. Fill glasses or bottles with different amounts of water. Experiment with the differences in sound produced by more or less water.

14. Color and Number Games. Draw a long, crooked, and crossed double line on a large piece of tagboard or other cardboard. Divide into small squares. Color the squares four different colors in random order. Use a spinner divided into four colors. Children can take turns spinning and moving a bottle top to the color the spinner lands on from the beginning to the end of the game. Do the same thing using numbers. With the number game dice can be used to determine how far to move.

15. Addition Wheels. Use cardboard from pizzas or any other round

cardboard that is stiff. Paint one side with the number to be added in the center and other numbers around it. Use a clothespin to mark the numbers to be added. Put correct answers on the back opposite the number.

16. Number Train. Draw an engine and caboose on cardboard and cut it out. Make cars with numbers 1–100. Prepare task cards such as "Make a train with cars numbered 1–111." or "Make a train with cars numbered 31–43." The task cards could also be made to use the train for addition.

17. Beanbag Toss. Use twelve or more cardboard pieces that differ in shape and color each with a number written on it. Arrange the pieces on the floor. The child throws the beanbag and names the number, color and shape it lands on.

18. Geoboards. Use a plywood square and 100 nails—10 rows or 10 nails. (Older children can make their own.) Children can use colored rubber bands or yarn to make designs.

You will be able to think of many more games or materials to use. There are also many books which provide ideas. Using games is a particularly appealing way to help children work on concepts being taught or to help a child who is having difficulty to comprehend a particular concept. Appendix C at the end of the book lists other sources of materials for classroom use.

NOTES

1. Ruth Phillips, "Doll Play as Function of the Realism of the Materials and the Length of the Experimental Session," *Child Development,* 16: 125–143, 1945.

2. Mary A. Pulaski, "The Rich Rewards of Make-Believe," *Psychology Today,* 6: 68–74, 1974.

3. Suzanne L. D. McFarland, "The Effects of Play and Toy Stereotypic Values on Associative Fluency of Kindergarten Children," (Unpublished Doctoral Dissertation, Indiana University), 1976.

4. Paul Hogan, *Playgrounds for Free* (Cambridge, Mass.: The MIT Press, 1974).

SPECIAL

APPLICATIONS

In previous chapters we discussed the way play develops and how adults can provide guidance and materials which aid development. We focused on typical behaviors and on procedures which can be tried with children whose growth is proceeding normally.

For most children there is a period when development does not proceed typically, and measures are necessary to correct their behavior. Chapter Eight describes the ways play can be used as a corrective activity for emotionally disturbed children and for children whose development is delayed.

It follows that if play assumes an important role in development, it should also assume an important role in the total educational program. In some educational programs, play provides a major vehicle for learning, but in others it is tolerated mostly because of the difficulty children have concentrating on academics for an entire school day without some break in activity. We feel that play should assume a very central role in a developmental school, and in Chapter Nine, we explain how play can contribute to the educational program of kindergarten and primary grades.

CHAPTER
EIGHT

Proper role performance often calls for skilled use of the whole body in a convincing show of poised balance and coordination.

Play as
Corrective Activity

This chapter will not teach you how to be a play therapist. But you will learn, among other things, what play therapy is, how it is conducted, what your role should be in cooperating with a child's therapist, and what play therapy techniques you may use to meet the special needs of your children and students. Our experience is that teachers and parents can become successful therapists if they receive direct supervision in actual therapy, but one does not learn how to conduct play therapy by reading a book. Doing therapy requires personal growth, which takes time, guidance, and support, and continuing experience as a therapist. Even after gaining experience, a therapist may encounter issues that require additional training and supervision. Furthermore, everyone of us is not necessarily capable of becoming a play therapist, no matter what our learning backgrounds are.

Do not feel disappointed that you will not be learning to do play therapy. An excessive amount of glamour has become attached to all forms of therapy in the minds of many people, and to play therapy in particular. You can take a larger perspective, that is, the prevention of problems is more important than treating problems. If problems can be prevented, both the affected persons and society are the ultimate beneficiaries. Therefore, if you as a teacher, parent, or child care worker can work to prevent a problem, your efforts are every bit as important as those of someone who treats children who have already developed disabling problems.

Until this chapter, play has been viewed as a generalized process which promotes normal development when children have the opportunity to be actively involved in what interests and challenges them at their individual development levels. So long as development proceeds normally, children tend to engage themselves actively in the process sufficiently to promote their development. That is, they are sufficiently motivated to play that they do develop. Children's automatic involvement in appropriate play constitutes the basis for allowing unplanned, spontaneous play to serve as a primary focus of many early childhood programs.

It is evident, however, that a surprising number of children exhibit forms of spontaneous play which are probably beneficial to them in some areas but which interfere with their development in other areas. For example, a child who is socially delayed in development may invest large amounts of time and energy in running, climbing, and playing on challenging equipment. The child, in other words, overemphasizes large motor activity because it is rewarding, and may thereby show advanced motor skills. But such an overinvestment in the motor area may be at the expense of needed involvement in different activities which promote communication and other social relationship skills. When this happens and is allowed to continue over many months and years, individual children drop further and further behind in particular areas of development. Eventually parts of their play become so obviously out of phase with the rest of their development that they are said to have a problem. These facts raise potentially serious ethical dilemmas for early childhood educators who refuse to rechannel or redirect children's behavior or to provide guidance, because their own views on "totally spontaneous development through play" interfere with their seeing and supplying what individual children actually need.

Throughout the book examples have been given of ways that adults should provide for children's play, guide them in their play, interact with them through play, model other forms of play, and show them how to manage resource materials. Thus, this book conceptualizes the adult role as an active and constructive one moderated by careful observation of children's needs and responsiveness to those needs. In this way, the adult does not intrude into the children's play; instead the adult intervenes naturally and unobtrusively. Care is taken not to dominate, overwhelm, intimidate or overshadow the play, thereby allowing the children to remain actively in control of their own activities.

With children who have special needs and are behind in some areas of development, the same general adult role is valid and workable. What changes is the focus, to play as corrective activity and to a greater emphasis on adults' actively promoting children's involvement in activities that are beneficial in view of their particular needs. For instance, children whose hand-eye coordination is delayed may be exposed to increased opportunities to engage in activities to develop these skills; at the same time the adult should make a special effort to insure that the corrective play activities are interesting and not too difficult. The children will still be able to choose, but for a part of the time the available choices should be perceptibly channeled toward ones that respond to their particular needs.

On the other hand, the laissez-faire role can prove detrimental for children with special needs. Some children simply do not improve or develop their potential competencies when left to their own devices. Most teachers have, for example, seen a child, more often a boy, who loves to chase around and engage in rough play, but who lacks the planning, communicating, and constructing skills to become involved in more mature and reproductive forms of play with other children. Children like this are allowed, in some preschool programs, to continue selecting large motor-oriented forms of social play almost exclusively—so long as the children do not become destructive and aggressive. If they are not helped to move beyond this level during the pre-school period, this form of play is a great hindrance to other forms of learning; it increasingly becomes a behavior problem if allowed to continue into the primary level program. In these instances, a rigid laissez-faire position on play is self-deceptive for the adult and potentially damaging for children.

Because the majority of children experience special developmental needs sometimes, the next section of this chapter examines how play can be used as corrective activity to meet the needs of all children. After this, we examine the use of play with emotionally disturbed children and the use of play with other developmentally disabled children.

As a Need of All Children

Development does not always proceed smoothly. It has its ups and downs. Little disturbances or interruptions of development are seen in nearly all children, and often they go away just as spontaneously as they come. Sometimes they do not.

Patterns of Special Needs. *Preschool.* We have studied the developmental patterns of a sizeable number of children, three through six years of age, by grouping their behaviors into five areas: large motor, social relations, self-help, language, and fine motor/academic skills.[1] Almost all children lag in at least one of these areas compared to their other areas. These lags often appear to be such that they interfere, in recognizable ways, with the child's own efforts to develop.

But even when the ups and downs of development seem likely to resolve themselves, the transition back to a more balanced pattern of development can often be facilitated and hastened by corrective play activity. It is also possible that temporary ups and downs in development last longer when there are fewer opportunities for corrective play. It may in fact be that some more seriously imbalanced, lifelong patterns of development originate this way. The child becomes locked in a cycle of relying heavily on certain more fully developed behaviors to the neglect of others, as in the earlier example of the child who overinvests in active, large motor play.

Primary. We have also studied areas in which many primary level children (K–2) show developmental lags.[2] The Division of Early Childhood of the Appalachia Educational Laboratory asked experienced kindergarten, first, and second grade teachers to judge the extent to which children they had taught were competent in each of these areas: relating to others socially, relating to adults, forming preferences, getting attention, responding to new things, motor, self-concept, perception, conceptual development, language, independence skills, number concepts, emotional expression, and self-control. (See Chapter Two for a more complete discussion of these areas.) It was possible to tell from these teacher ratings whether, for example, kindergarten children tend to have greater developmental lags than other children. Lags can occur, of course, in any and all areas for individual children, but on the average the lags are more pronounced in particular areas of development. This knowledge can help you to plan systematically for areas which affect many children.

Based on these findings, it appears that by entrance into kindergarten, children are most advanced in relating to adults, although some significant numbers of children continue to have special needs around the issues of trust, autonomy, and initiative.

A majority of children, although fewer than for "relating to adults," are competent in emotional expression, motor development, attention getting, self-concept, self-control, relating to peers, and forming preferences. Special provision is needed, however, in each of these areas for a sizeable minority of children within any typical group.

An even larger minority of kindergarten children has special developmental needs in perception and language, responding to new things, and developing independence skills.

Kindergarten teachers find that a majority of children need experiences which will lead to further conceptual development and particularly development of number concepts.

The demands of first and second grades differ from those of kindergarten, as most child care workers are aware. Children experience new expectations from both school and home, often communicated with a sense of urgency. In some ways, therefore, the movement from kindergarten to first grade stimulates the appearance of developmental needs which were less evident before that time.

For the reasons we have just cited, many first graders need renewed opportunities to develop fine motor skills, and improve relations with adults both of which actually appear to be less mature than they were a year earlier!

An even more overwhelming minority of first graders needs further experiences contributing to development in perception, language, and forming preferences. Not surprisingly, under the stress of first grade "culture shock," many children seem to regress or become less skillful, compared to kindergarten, in the following areas: emotional expression, maturity of attention getting, self-concept, independence skills, self-control, and relating to peers. In recognition of these changes, first grade classrooms need to provide special learning opportunities for perhaps over forty percent of all children. It is probably also true that reorienting the first grade to the preferred learning capacities of children, as called for throughout this book and especially in Chapter Nine, can do much to prevent such regressive behavior from occurring.

The preceding suggestion receives some support from our findings in the same study for second graders. In every major area of development, second graders were judged by their teachers to be more mature on the average than first grade teachers judged their children to be. This probably results from the process of gradually and directly adjusting to school and its new demands and expectations. But in spite of the improvement in all developmental areas, substantial percentages of second graders demonstrate ongoing special developmental needs.

An overall rough estimate, across all areas of development, suggests that about one-third of all second graders still have ongoing special needs. The actual percentage is probably higher than this, because lags in one area are not necessarily associated with lags in other areas.

Second graders appear to achieve their greatest competency in motor and independence skills. Only a small proportion of children in each group is likely to have special needs in these areas.

A somewhat larger minority of second graders have lags and need special assistance with their development in these areas: perception, emotional expression, attention getting behaviors, self-concept, self-control, peer relations, relations with adults, and forming preferences.

An even larger minority of second graders is behind in these areas: number concepts, language, and responding to new things. Finally, general conceptual development lags even further behind as judged by experienced teachers.

When comparisons are made from the teacher ratings between kindergarten and second grade children's developmental progress, the overall sense is that they hold their own or progress slightly. By second grade, progress is especially noticeable in fine motor, perception, independence skills, general conceptual development, and number concepts. A decline is suggested only in the area of relating to adults. This last fact may accurately reflect the extent to which second graders are becoming more oriented to pleasing peers and, in consequence, less oriented toward and conforming to adults.

Thus, from kindergarten to second grade children do progress. Moreover, they recover from the shock of first grade and generally become more happy, capable, and productive within just one year. But the successful transition from preschool into primary for some children is mixed with the agonies of the one-third or more children who still are not making it in the classroom. What must be remembered is that the delays occur in primary level classrooms, as they are presently organized within schools. What is encouraging in the face of these facts, is that teachers and other child care workers can make a difference. Further, special needs can be met through a more activity-oriented primary school as presented in Chapter Nine.

So far we have reviewed two studies of competency development and lag, one among preschoolers (3-6 years) and one regarding primary level children (K-2nd). These serve to establish a basis in fact for saying that developmental activities, including play, are needs of children throughout these years. Now we can return to the theme presented at the beginning of this section, namely, that simple and temporary lags in certain areas of development may become lasting ones. This claim is supported by our finding that a large percentage of second graders show significant lags in selected developmental areas.

Planning Corrective Play

Given the need of many normal children for corrective play activity, the question is how the adult can proceed with planning. We can answer this question by considering several areas: creating a climate for play, the adult-child relationship, determining areas of individual need, and arranging the play environment. The same general guidelines apply to planning corrective play for emotionally disturbed and developmentally delayed children.

Creating a Climate for Play. Corrective play requires a special climate. Play is usually a tentative activity in the sense that the child can try things out without having to maintain or keep them that way. An emphasis on doing things "the correct way" effectively undermines and destroys this tentative quality. To call play tentative does not mean that it cannot be serious or intense, because it can be both. But adults often think that something cannot be both tentative or playful and simultaneously be serious or intense. Thus, some adults have concepts that stand in the way of their emotional acceptance of the nature and values of play. The crucial adult attitude in this regard is one of accepting play for what it is.

A second aspect of climate is that play is chosen rather than assigned. In addition, it may be self-initiated, but self-initiation is not a necessary feature of play. For example, when one child initiates play and another child responds, the second child indeed plays, even though not the initiator of play. Thus, to create a climate for play it is necessary to include an element of choice. The choice need not be totally open-ended—life's choices seldom are. Neither must the choice be among highly favored alternatives, but the choice must appear attractive or at least acceptable. For example, a child who is being encouraged to try out some new activities which relate to independence skills development might be offered three relevant choices, and have their attractive aspects pointed out. Finally, offering choices need not be by spoken words;

it is enough that alternatives be physically present, although verbally offered choices remain a possibility. It should be noted that, given limited choices, a verbal statement may draw attention to the fact that the adult is setting limits on the range of possible options. For instance, if virtually all of the accessible activities for a given day tend to encourage relating to other children socially, it will be unnecessary to talk much about the options available. By paying attention to these considerations, adults can offer limited choices that include ones which relate to the child's needs, but which the child might otherwise ignore.

Play is, furthermore, intrinsically motivating and internally motivated; children play because they are challenged by an activity and can perceive it as possibly enjoyable. Children cannot be rewarded for playing or bribed to play. Playing provides its own reward and meaning; to reward is to destroy. Children can, however, have certain forms of play made perceptibly more attractive through modeling. This can be done by your demonstrating what can be done, using particular play materials. When someone else is obviously enjoying an activity, it increases in attractiveness. Thus, it must be all right to enjoy or to have fun. Sometimes adults are confused; they think that learning cannot be enjoyable. Children know better. They learn little on their own unless it can be made enjoyable.

The Adult-Child Relationship. The adult who is congruent with all of the aspects of climate needs to communicate this congruence. It may not be perceived automatically by young children. To communicate congruence means to enter so much into the climate of play yourself, that children can tell from your whole attitude: *(a)* you accept their play and value it, *(b)* you really want them to have choices and you also want them to try new things, and *(c)* you believe that play and learning are enjoyable. Sometimes adults have to work at this. In the process, they may discover that a lack of congruence in one of these aspects is in fact interfering with communication of climate.

Just as play must be accepted, the child must be accepted. This may mean accepting a child's initially lukewarm response to choices being offered, and trying to find out what would make the choices more appealing. If the adult sets limits on the child's choices, this should happen in an atmosphere of acceptance. Otherwise the child feels, "You don't want me to have any fun" or "You don't like me."

Acceptance between adult and child works better in an active rather than a passive mode. That is, the adult should show interest in, observe, and remark or ask questions about what the child is doing. As the adult communicates a genuine interest in what the child is doing, this says to the child, "I like you."

The adult-child relationship in play allows the child to feel accepted. It must also be a relationship in which the adult honestly reflects personal values and orientations. That is, the adult does not adjust totally to the child's frame of reference any more than the child is expected to adjust to the adult's frame of reference. In this kind of relationship the adult has as much freedom as the child to speak forthrightly. The secret lies not in submerging your values, but in expressing them in a loving and accepting way. For example, there is a great difference between the following adult statements: "I wish you wouldn't do that," and "You know, I think we don't have as much fun when we do things like that."

An effective adult-child relationship in play also includes an element of mutual enjoyment. If individual children sense that an adult enjoys being around them, they realize that they are accepted. The relationship is mutual. It is also all right for the child to enjoy the adult.

When the adult and child enjoy each other's companionship, it is natural for them to enjoy what they do together. In this way, the positive relationship of child and adult can add a positive attraction to performing activities that might otherwise be ignored by the child.

In relating, the adult needs to find ways to be a partner and model in play without taking over or dominating the play. Being aware of your own goals and needs is important in this regard. When you feel a sense of urgency or pressure about how things are going in play, you are on the verge of becoming intrusive. The private message you need to give yourself is, "Take it easy. This is play after all. I have to hold onto the serious but tentative quality of play."

To be unobtrusive in the play relationship means to be natural and in touch with the purpose of the play itself. The intrinsic purpose of play is always to carry out whatever the play involves. Play's purpose is, therefore, not play's goal. Play's goal is the special meaning that you as an adult can give to play. You can say, for example, the child is building with construction materials to become competent in motor skills. This is true. But the focus of play for the child must remain on its immediate purpose and not its remote goal. Only the immediate purpose is intrinsically motivating.

The adult is in a position to understand the more remote implications of the child's play, the goals of play. Further, the adult can recognize when there is an imbalance in the child's play with a consequent loss of opportunities to try other potentially interesting possibilities, as discussed earlier in this chapter. In the adult-child relationship, the adult accepts the responsibility for thinking through the connections between the concrete actions of play and the goals of growing up and being a competent human being. But always the responsibility must be carried lightly and patiently so that it does not intrude upon the immediate, concrete reality of play. That is, play must be guided but without any feeling of urgency or pressure.

These, in summary, are some of the ingredients of the adult-child relationship in play: acceptance, mutual enjoyment, being a nondominating partner, and remaining in touch with the immediate purpose of play, while guiding play toward its more remote goals. Probably doing all of this requires that the adult have a strong personal capacity for play.

Determining Areas of Individual Need. There are many ways of analyzing individual children's needs for play. Some form of systematic observation and recording is essential. There will be an element of personal judgment in this, based on the adult's experience. The richer this experience, the more the adult will be able to use insights from other children to understand the child in question. Judicious use of simple developmental tests or screening tests can be extremely useful. It is never enough, however, to test and compare the child to others. The appraisal must ultimately focus on the internal organization and directions of movement among the various areas of the individual child's development.

The areas of development, that we have already discussed in this chapter, will help you to strive for a comprehensive view of individual children's progress. Try thinking, for example, of the child's needs in the areas of communications, social skills, conceptual skills, motor development, and self-help. It is not necessary, however, to use the preceding list of five areas. What matters most is that you choose some method of observing your children's progress across all areas of development, and then use it.

It will be necessary to form some impression of those areas in which the child is progressing more rapidly and less rapidly. If you keep records of these impressions, you can refer to them later to evaluate progress. Often it will be possible to provide forms of play in which the child will need to perform behaviors relating to both more rapidly and less rapidly developing areas. This process will insure that individual children gain needed experience that calls on their more slowly developing competencies. In this way, some restoration of balance may occur.

Arranging the Environment. A learning center which emphasizes play is a dynamic environment. It is forever changing. Types of material that lend themselves to particular forms of play will be rotated in and out. Thus, storage is required to keep some materials out of sight and reach, and attention should also be given to the overall physical arrangement. Play areas calling for more or less compatible forms of activity, such as quiet areas or noisy areas, can be arranged near each other. This reduces the risk of having unwanted activities spill over into other areas.

Whenever limits must be set, a simple sign in a primary classroom can convey the message. For example, "Limit: 4 Children" or "Play Quietly Here" or "Take Turns." Businesslike signs can be used as reminders, and form a focal point for discussion with individual children who have problems remembering.

Some early childhood programs have successfully used simple plans for rotating children in and out of certain areas. The necessary feature is a method of either keeping records (e.g., charts) or regulating children's movement (e.g., tokens which can be used to gain entrance to similarly color-coded areas. It is usual to have related areas similarly coded, so that there are always some choices available.) The frequency with which available areas are rearranged and individual schedules changed will depend on such considerations as class size, available space, the interest span of the children, and length of the program day/week.

The individual assessment of needs is used to plan a recommended mix of activities for each child. A key word here is *recommended.* The adult leader may, accordingly, make changes in the child's plan as required by the circumstances. It is also a good idea to provide for free choices within any scheduling system. For example, a child might be given the chance to schedule one or two more "red" or "green" or "blue" activities, as desired. One special risk of these arrangements is that rotation times will come too frequently or too abruptly. You will need to observe the children closely to become aware of how long their attention spans are for different kinds of activities. We will examine, here, some ways of managing transitions effectively. First, rules of thumb are not as helpful for planning transitions as careful observation of how the children's activities progress. An activity should normally be allowed to continue long enough for children to feel they have accomplished some of their immediate purposes and interrupted before children begin to lose interest and become restless. Reaching a desirable balance across several areas will require that you take care not to rush children out of one play area just because those in another area are restless. Nearly all children cope with transitions a little better if they know in advance what is about to happen. Various signals can serve to announce transitions, e.g., temporarily dimming lights, turning on recorded transition music, or having a child silently display a small sign in each area, "5 more minutes." Transitions are easier, too, if children have a clear idea of when they may next return to what they are about to leave, and if they can be assured that their products will be preserved or reinstated at a later time. For example, if there are enough blocks that some of them can be left out, a child's block work might be left in place with a cardboard box placed over it to protect it. The box might have a "Stop" sign painted on top of it.

Chapter Seven and Appendix C indicate the kinds of materials which can be used to arrange the environment to permit certain kinds of activity to occur. When used imaginatively, their practical guidance will take you far along the way toward achieving the activities mix which your group of children needs.

Conducting Corrective Play

If you have understood and carried out the suggestions made up to this point, you are ready to conduct corrective play for normal children. When you do, many expected and some unexpected things will happen. Not only is the play environment dynamic, the process of guiding children in such an environment is also dynamic. You need to be prepared for all occurrences, so you will not become overly concerned when things do not proceed according to plan.

Suppose that your plan operates at only 25 percent efficiency at first. Is that bad? Or is it good? Since it would seem to be a 25 percent improvement over unplanned use of the play environment, it must be good. This line of reasoning should make you feel a little more comfortable about gradually getting the feel of what it is like to conduct corrective play.

Not every child will have a planned, corrective play schedule. The schedules for those children who show fairly balanced development across areas will be based on the choices they would normally make in the present environment.

It will be important for you to have a sense of timing in relation to individual children's progress. Competency improvement in lagging areas tends to proceed slowly. The first signs of progress may be a growing interest plus the child's enjoyment of new types of activity that were formerly ignored. Further progress in the associated competencies will appear following this change. It is enough that you will see some progress.

While the children are busy playing, you can be moving quietly about the play area. You will be looking for those little situations which inevitably arise calling for your guidance and active involvement. For example, two children may want the same materials at the same time. You may have to intervene, but you must give them a chance to work out their own solution. Next, you will observe what is happening among the groups of children in each play activity area: whether they have the materials they need, and whether they are entering into play activities which draw on the special potentials of that area. Finally, you will want to notice what is happening with individual children in each area, and perhaps to make some observational notes. Thus, your attention should shift continually back and forth as you adopt the three preceding frames of reference.

Another essential feature of your work will be to provide a continually revolving, interesting variety of resources for the children. Whenever a child needs more fine motor experience, for example, the child's willingness to engage in greater quantities of fine motor play will depend upon the availability of stimulating resources. Your own direct involvement in the children's play can enhance greatly the variety of uses to which children can put the available materials. If you work in these ways to provide corrective play activities to those children who need them, you will be helping to prevent more serious developmental problems. You will, further, be helping children to develop the widest possible array of competencies.

Play with Emotionally Disturbed Children

Individual Therapy. The traditional and most familiar use of corrective therapy is with children who are emotionally disturbed. Play therapy has most typically been conducted with one child in a small playroom with an adult, the therapist, present. Play therapists are usually persons trained in psychiatry or psychology, and sometimes in pediatrics, social work, counseling, and recreation. They have a variety of theoretical views. But whatever theories they follow, they tend to view play therapy as a means to *(a)* assist the child in communicating with and relating to the therapist, *(b)* provide an outlet or medium through which the child can express problems and feelings, and *(c)* permit the child to develop more normally. Before discussing play therapy further, we should note that emotionally disturbed children can be treated by several other methods besides play therapy, e.g., drug therapy, behavior modification, and structured environments.

The first impression many people get of play therapy is that it has to do primarily with children's releasing pent-up emotions and frustrations. This happens, of course, but not as commonly as the popular notion suggests. It is more common for children to deal with the same themes repeatedly, like a phonograph needle stuck on a broken record.

The play of disturbed children is always immature in some respects, even when their overall ability levels are average or above average. For example, a prominent amount of early sensory play activity will often be seen in their play although the child might otherwise be able to participate in reproductive play or games with rules. No single description of disturbed children's play would be adequate, however, because the term *emotionally disturbed* is a broad categorical name for children who display a great variety of differing behavioral patterns.

Play therapy means many things beyond the three shared purposes previously mentioned. It is conducted in a variety of ways depending upon the therapist's theoretical frame of reference. The therapist may be fairly active in the play or may be mainly an observer. The therapist may discuss the meaning of the child's behavior from time to time or focus on the play itself or on the therapeutic relationship.

Materials favored for play therapy by most therapists are those which allow the child's imagination greater reign or provide ready outlets for the child's feelings. Mechanical toys, which do something for the child to observe, are poor play therapy materials. Typical play materials include: sand, water, clay, arts and crafts materials, construction materials, dolls, hand puppets, guns, games, and such. Occasionally, children may be allowed to bring some of their own materials into the play session.

Group Therapies. Besides individual play therapy, group therapy is practiced with disturbed children. This form of therapy is little known to the general public. As with individual therapy, group therapy is conducted in several ways. Each form of group therapy tends to relate to the particular theory on which it is based.

A specialized form of group therapy practiced by one of the writers of this text is called *sibling group therapy* in which children from the same family group are seen together. One or both parents may be involved in the group from time to time, and if the parents are present, it is called *conjoint family therapy.* In the sibling group, if the children are all ten to twelve years or older, play is usually not used; instead, the method of interaction is discussion, role playing, games, and various forms of psychodrama. If most of the children in the sibling group are preschool and primary age, then sibling group play therapy is employed in a playroom with the usual kinds of play materials. When parents are not in the group, they may be on the other side of a one-way mirror learning to better observe what is going on with their children.

The purposes of sibling group play therapy are the same as those of individual play therapy plus a few other goals. The other goals are: *(a)* to deal through play with the roles, interpersonal relations, and communications that exist in the sibling group and *(b)* to lay a more positive foundation for the lifelong relations that siblings will have with one another. When parents are present in the play sessions, a further purpose is to show and give the parents practice in relating to their children through their play.

These brief comments provide some sense of what individual and group forms of play therapy are and how they are conducted. The section immediately preceding this section has, in addition, considered how the more general techniques and orientations of individual play therapy apply to working with the developmental needs of normal children. A further word is needed here regarding the application of group play therapy approaches with normal children.

Teachers and other child care workers will normally be working with children in groups. Individual play therapy provides a useful example for individual developmental needs appraisal and planning; group play therapy provides a workable example for analyzing the interpersonal relations and communications that occur during play. Occasionally, siblings will be present in the same classroom or program. At such time, the added perspectives of sibling and parent roles within the family may be helpful to the child care worker.

Children who are in your classroom or program may be in play therapy as well. In these instances, you need to know how to relate to and cooperate with the child's therapist. Minimally, if the child's parents consent to it, you and the therapist should share information on your goals and methods. Each should help the other understand what the child will be experiencing in each setting. More than this may happen. Some therapists may want you to observe whether certain things are happening when the child is with you. Collaboration may go beyond this to working closely together to help the child. Other therapists may want nothing more than a little information exchange. Therapists differ in this respect just as their therapies and theories differ.

Play with Developmentally Delayed Children

The term, *developmentally delayed,* is becoming somewhat more familiar, but a little explanation is needed. It does not mean mentally retarded, although mentally retarded children are among the developmentally delayed. It means any of a variety of unrelated conditions which cause children to experience significant delay in important areas of development. Hearing loss, loss of sight, motor handicaps, and mental retardation are some of the conditions associated with significant developmental delay.

Play therapy has traditionally not been used with children having retarded development; however, blind children are sometimes treated using child psychoanalysis. More recently considerable interest has been expressed in using play as corrective activity with children who experience developmental delay as a result of a variety of handicapping conditions.

Unfortunately, some enthusiasts seem to expect that unplanned play will work magically to meet the needs of exceptional children. The fact is that, the more exceptional the children are, the less likely it is that unplanned play will meet their special needs. That is, extra planning is needed to meet the needs of developmentally delayed children through play. One reason for this is that very exceptional children often are not internally motivated to engage in some of the very activities which could most help them develop.

Nevertheless, corrective play has much to offer to exceptional children, when it is offered as a part of an overall planned program for the individual child. Accordingly, there have been instances where individually trained and supervised teachers, social workers, and psychometrists provide play as corrective activity for very exceptional developmentally delayed children. These experiences have shown that *(a)* these kinds of child care workers, when carefully selected for training, can learn to be corrective play therapists, and *(b)* very exceptional children benefit from the play activities which the therapists provide.

Thus, a new frontier appears to be opening. Perhaps in the future corrective play activities, based on careful appraisal and planning for individual needs, will be used to meet the developmental needs of nearly all children.

NOTES

1. Edward E. Gotts, *Form for Rating Attainment of Early Childhood Competencies and Behavioral Performances,* (Charleston, West Virginia: Appalachia Educational Laboratory, 1975).

2. Edward E. Gotts, Del Lawhon, and Alice M. Spriggs, *Final Report: Marketable Preschool Education, 1975–76,* (Charleston, West Virginia, Appalachia Educational Laboratory, 1976).

CHAPTER
NINE

*To live in a rapidly changing environment,
children and adults must be adaptable
and capable of coping with change.*

Toward a Developmental Primary School (K-3)

An educational program which is timely takes into account both the skills of the learner and the demands of the world in which the learner lives. This means that in planning an educational program for young children today we must consider our rapidly changing society and the demands that it will make on these children. Since young children are present rather than future oriented, adults responsible for planning educational programs must project ahead to some of the characteristics that will serve children well in the future. The planning task is to provide a present which is relevant to the future but which at the same time is consistent with the developing abilities of young children.

One of children's developing abilities is play. But play is more than this. It is a "grand strategy" whereby the child develops many other abilities, that is, a means of learning. In previous chapters we described the role of play and how it can be used to promote development. In this chapter, we shall describe a developmental primary school (which uses play as an important learning medium), why we should have a developmental school, and the role of play in the curriculum. We shall focus primarily on play in the kindergarten-primary program, because play has been widely accepted in nursery school programs and has been widely utilized in programs for children under five years of age. The ages of five and six are crucial, because at this time, children begin to feel most strongly the impact of what society expects. The pressure to eliminate play and get on with the business of learning academic skills is strongly felt by most children during their early school years.

Why a Developmental School

Much controversy in early childhood education is related to which educational experiences should be provided for young children and how they should be organized. Related to the role of play in early childhood education is the issue of whether we should organize a particular body of material which is then taught to children or whether the curriculum should evolve, at least in part, from the young child's direct experience. The organization of play comes from within the child and reflects the child's development, experiences and unique way of organizing and responding to them. Therefore, play has an important role in a developmental primary school.

When many young children today enter school they experience a form of "culture shock." School expectations are noticeably different from their previous experiences. Although many of these school experiences are based on a hypothetical definition of a five or six year old, they may have little relevance to the particular abilities of any individual child. The attempt is often made to teach some children to read without prior experiences with reading or with other areas of development which would prepare them for reading. Some children who already know how to read do not encounter either experiences or materials that further stimulate this skill. With either problem children experience a terrible waste of abilities. One problem arises out of failure and the other arises from lack of stimulation. These are tragic losses.

Cultural shock does not happen only because of discrepancies between what is taught and the child's cognitive development. It also arises from the social and physical expectations made for the child. Children who have been physically active for most of the day may be expected to be still and quiet for the time they are in school. Children who have been functioning on their own schedule are often expected to adjust to an inflexible class schedule. Children who have had their own toys and full attention from their mothers are expected to share both materials and the teacher's attention with other children. Not all of the shock can be avoided, but a developmental school could reduce it considerably. For example, in Chapter Four we discussed how to reduce some of the social shock in adjusting to the school environment.

Another reason for having a developmental school is to take advantage of the child's intrinsic motivation. In Chapter Three we described some of the child's tireless efforts to explore the physical environment. The advantage of the developmental school that we refer to here comes from its deliberate effort to introduce things into the environment to "turn the child on" as opposed to trying to stimulate interest in a predetermined curriculum. Only when we supply a variety of materials and learning experiences and provide the child with opportunities to choose what to do, can we expect to capitalize on the child's natural interest and curiosity about things and desire to learn.

Taking advantage of intrinsic motivation is partially a matter of planning for individual children to be successful. Whether it is in the regulation of attention (Chapters Three and Five), the persistence in play (Chapter Four), or the use of imagination (Chapter Six), continuation of the activity is dependent upon a feeling of satisfaction or success. There is comparatively little failure in a developmental school. At least, failures are far overshadowed by success.

In Chapter Five, we described the role of play in the child's developing individuality and how the young child's self-concept can be changed by early school experiences. This change most likely will be in a positive direction if the curriculum and the teacher's expectations can be adjusted in terms of the child's development. Growth usually proceeds in a positive way so long as children are provided experiences which are stimulating yet within the realm of their abilities. Experiences which are too difficult lead to failure and possible loss of self-esteem. The development of a positive self-concept is an important goal of a developmental school.

Goals for a Developmental School

Planning the goals for a developmental school requires that we keep in mind the kind of society in which today's children live. As previously mentioned, this society is marked by rapid and far-reaching economic and social change. In the future, society probably will provide an even wider choice of goods and services than are available today. People may be called upon to change their occupations with greater frequency. Changes in the industrial work week could result in greater amounts of leisure and recreational time for all. We can hope that it will create a caring environment as well as one that is stimulating, honest, and tolerant.

With this kind of society in mind, we propose four very broad goals for the developmental school. To:

1. Provide for the development of adaptive behavior
2. Provide a curriculum which is balanced across affective, cognitive, and physical areas
3. Provide for the development of basic skills required for full participation in society
4. Help the child acquire a future-focused, self-evolving role image.

These goals need considerable discussion because they are different from those usually stated for primary education. They also must be defined in terms of how they relate to the young child's learning.

Development of Adaptable Behavior. In order to live in a rapidly changing environment, children and adults must above all be adaptable and capable of coping with changes in that environment. We believe that a school which utilizes a play environment for learning provides children with some of the experiences needed for developing adaptability. A play situation, particularly an elaborate sociodramatic play situation, requires a high degree of adapt-ability. Children must adjust to both the behavior of other children and to the unknown aspects of the outcome of the play. The developmental school provides opportunities for making real choices in supervised situations and provides the children with the opportunity to learn from their mistakes. Children have opportunities to think independently and to behave responsibly.

The school should help children develop positive self-concepts. Beginning with their earliest experiences, children should be helped to think of them-selves as worthwhile. They learn to know themselves and to accept themselves as persons with strengths and limitations. They must like and feel good about themselves and have a general feeling of confidence, particularly in their ability to solve problems. Play presents the opportunity for solving many simple and complex problems. It allows children to experience success at a time when they cannot be successful in many real world situations. Only if children acquire confidence and stability, will they be able to withstand the increasing pressures of a changing society, and only then will they possess the internal flexibility to be truly adaptable.

Children must learn how to learn, because adaptability is the result of having within oneself the tools for effecting personal change and progress. It is possible that in the future change will occur with such rapidity that people will be required to retool themselves for new and different occupations as their skills become outmoded. Learning how to learn is an extension of the young child's curiosity. It includes both the desire to find out about things and the skills to do so. The developmental school should help children learn how to learn, think of learning as worthwhile and view it as a lifelong process.

Balance in the Curriculum. The school program should recognize and build upon the interrelatedness of all development. We should continue, of course, to be concerned about the information and concepts that children are learning, but the fact that children need assistance in all developmental areas indicates that we should emphasize the affective and physical areas of development as well.

If we refer again to the first objective, the development of adaptive behav-ior, we find that balance in affective, cognitive and physical areas of the curriculum is basic. Many of the characteristics essential to adaptability are in the affective domain. We mentioned the role of play in developing positive self-concepts and in learning how to learn. A further requirement is the development of resourcefulness and initiative based upon experiences of successfully creating with materials and ideas, such as with art media, songs and rhythms, dramatics, storytelling, and creative writing. Children must create a personal world for themselves in which they have ideas for things they want to do and the skills and abilities to accomplish their goals. They must learn to use leisure time to create and re-create rather than to be bored.

With the advent of the "jet age," access by many people to other parts of the world is already a reality. Our need to live peaceably with people of very different backgrounds both at home and abroad is already deeply felt. Schools need to provide children with the abilities to live with others, appreciate and respect their differences, understand their feelings, and communicate effectively with them. As children interact with one another they should be helped to express sympathy and concern for other children and to value their own opinions in making decisions and solving problems.

If we again think in terms of the future, it is preferable for children to see themselves as cooperative rather than competitive. This is a departure from our earlier traditions which placed greater stress on individually-oriented competition than on group-oriented collaboration and achievement. One beginning step in this direction is to help children understand how other people respond to their behavior and how they respond to the behavior of others. The potential of play for contributing to such learning was discussed in Chapter Five.

Strong emphasis should be placed on learning about the physical environment. Much information is acquired and concepts developed through learning about the environment. It is also the area in which curiosity can be stimulated and in which some of the skills of learning how to learn can be acquired.

Physical and motor skills would be more strongly emphasized in the developmental school than in many present day schools as contributors to good physical health and to good motor coordination. The development of gross motor coordination is a prerequisite to successful participation in childhood games and the beginning skills needed for later participation in many kinds of sports. Hopefully, this would prevent many of today's drop-outs from the physical activity and fitness so necessary to participation in recreational activity. The development of fine motor coordination is a prerequisite to writing and to much creative activity in language, music, art, crafts, and other forms of creative self-expression.

Taking personal responsibility for sound health and nutritional habits also would be a vital part of this emphasis. Such an emphasis is now conceded to be a national priority. Only those citizens who are equipped for life by a balanced curriculum will have the necessary personal vitality and resilience to handle the rapid life changes which the future may bring.

Development of Basic Academic Skills. The need for better academic skills increases yearly because of the need to learn more things faster. Children must continue to acquire good academic skills to keep up with the knowledge explosion and their need for continued learning. In the developmental school, both timing and emphasis are different, but this goal is no less important. Teaching children to read, for example, would be a long-range goal, not an immediate goal. Reading would not be emphasized regardless of readiness and needed curricular balance for five and six year olds. Some children would acquire academic skills earlier than others because these aspects of their development occur earlier. Children with a slower developmental pace in language and perceptual skills would not be pressured into reading; they would be introduced to reading when they are ready. But eventually all children would learn to read unless they were hindered by specific learning disorders. This contrasts with today's alarmingly high, functional illiteracy rate among adults resulting from a nondevelopmental approach to basic skills. Academic skills would be used by the teacher and the children during play activities so that the need to acquire them is real and provides a definite sense of satisfaction.

Acquiring a Future-Focused Role-Image. Futurists are very critical of today's education which they describe as built on the model of past industrial bureaucracy. They maintain that a focus on the future is relevant to all learners, regardless of age, in order to provide both a motive and a means to achievement. The majority of middle class parents have a future-focused role-image for their children which they convey to them at an early age. Many parents, who are themselves unemployed or employed at such a low income level that they worry about whether their children will be fed and clothed, are so present-oriented that they cannot project a future-focused role-image to their children. To provide options for such children, schools can extend help to make them more aware of occupational areas previously unknown to them. In addition to taking children into the community to learn about different occupations, teachers can make maximum use of media and sociodramatic play to help children role play their observations of different occupations. Children also enjoy discussions about what they want to be when they grow up. New and possible occupations can be introduced into such discussions, thus promoting greater awareness of future roles without violating the child's more prominent present orientation. (For additional views on how a developmental school contributes to these and other aspects of self-identity development, see Chapter Five.)

Organization of a Developmental School

A developmental primary school has some similarities to the open classroom school but includes dimensions not often included in open classroom programs. Each school would have a high degree of autonomy. Administrators would foster openness and cooperation between faculty and administration, and between school and home. For the school to operate otherwise would defeat its purpose, because adults would not be able to model these behaviors for observation by the children. A faculty would be needed with particularly mature attitudes toward developmental learning, individual differences, and parent involvement. To keep the process open and adaptive all school personnel would require an exceptional ability to examine their own beliefs and strengths, and to make decisions based on this information in terms of the needs and abilities of the children. In other words, individual faculty would have to be able to function on the basis of how their own particular abilities fit into the total school resources rather than on the basis of individual wants and preferences. Although when needed, wants and preferences would be appropriately used.

Parents would be involved in several ways in the developmental school. This involvement would be necessary, not just to conform to guidelines or to a climate of opinion regarding its importance, but because the school could not function without it. Parent involvement would be necessary and actively sought to accomplish certain specified ends. Parents need to understand the organization and purposes of this approach to primary level educational operation, and they need to see specifically how this approach applies to their child's individual needs and progress. Parents need to be taught how to help their children develop as they progress through these early school years, and opportunities need to be provided for parents for training to further their children's development. Conversely, failure to provide for parent involvement to these ends would surely result in much misunderstanding and dissatisfaction, as parents compare the developmental school with the more traditional primary school that they themselves experienced. Failure to provide for parent involvement would make it likely that many parents would be unable to help their children as much as they otherwise might.

Admission and Grouping. Admission would be in the fall just as in a traditional school at approximately five years of age. The developmental school would require no special admission policy. Since the program would be adjusted to individual children, there would be no reason for early admissions. Neither would early admissions be ruled out. The school would be an ideal placement for children with certain handicaps although decisions would have to be made separately for the individual child.

There would be a preenrollment in the spring, and parents who enrolled children would be asked to bring them to visit the school before it was out in the spring. The teacher would observe the children during the visit and make notes on each one's behavior. Prior to placement in a class, teachers would interview parents regarding the children's previous experiences at home and in nursery school (or a child care center if they had previously been enrolled in a group setting). Children would then be placed in the classroom which provided the level of experience which seemed best suited to their individual development. This procedure unquestionably has an advantage over the random placement of children commonly practiced at most schools.

After the entry year, grouping into classes would be a matter for faculty decision. The children would be grouped into classes based upon their individual characteristics and based upon who among the faculty would most likely be a successful teacher for them. Teachers would be expected to keep good records on their children, including information which could lead to the best placement for each child. Placement would usually be for a school year although changes could be made during the school year if they were indicated. Keeping children in the same classroom for a year would not, however, be an arbitrary calendar-related convenience; it would be in recognition of the need most young children have to be given the opportunity over a considerable period of time to relate to the same group of familiar children and adults.

Grouping would be reconsidered at the end of each school year. Children might stay in one room for a year or they might stay there for two years. On some occasions a child might stay in a room for a third year. Most children would be with others not more than one year older or one year younger than they are. The age range in classes would differ but there would be overlap. For example, one class might include five, six and seven year olds. Another class might include just five and six year olds or six and seven year olds. In addition to chronological age, children would be grouped on the basis of social and emotional growth and school adjustment to provide the most desirable situation to meet their needs. For example, teachers should be able to identify children who demand an unfair amount of the teacher's time, those who seem to give stability to other children, those who have always been the youngest in their family and in their class, and those who seem to need the kind of classroom provided by a particular teacher. Children with like problems or like behavior most likely would not be placed together. These are examples of very subjective criteria for grouping, but teachers who have worked with children for at least a year would most likely have some hunches that would contribute to a better than random grouping. Children would always maintain an identity with a class and a teacher although there would be planned interactions among children in different classes.

During the parts of the day when children engage in choice or play activities, they can choose their playmates or those with whom they will work. Generally children would work or play with different children for different activities and at different times of the day. Total class activities would be kept to a minimum. Some assigned work would be done in committees as soon as children could assume this kind of responsibility. At times children would be encouraged to work independently. There would not be a system of formalized groups within a classroom.

Staffing. Many teachers, fully qualified to teach primary children, would not be able to function in the indirect and facilitating role required by the developmental school. To be successful the teachers must genuinely believe in the philosophy of the school and the importance of the developmental abilities of the children. Further, the teacher must trust in the children's desire to learn and to be socially accepted, because there will be many times when teachers will be called upon to support or defend what or how they are teaching.

The teacher must believe strongly in the value of direct experience— children handling materials and doing things for themselves as opposed to being told what happens when something is done. Not only must there be a strong belief in direct experience, but there must be a willingness to let children make some choices from among several options. The teacher must be energetic and resourceful to make certain the children do have appropriate choices.

To be effective in a developmental school the teacher must be able to relate warmly to children so they feel liked and secure. This security also includes the ability to establish limits of acceptable behavior. This task is not as easy as in a more authoritarian situation, because the teacher must not only see that the limits are set, but must also involve the children to the extent that they are able to participate. Teachers must adjust their expectations of compliance to the abilities of the specific children involved. Considering the specifics of the limits, the good of the class, and the good of an individual child is never easy and such decisions must constantly be made. Judgments must also be made about when to enforce a limit even though it will be difficult for the teacher and for the child.

The teacher must have a better than usual understanding of appropriate curricula for young children. Since the developmental school involves fitting the curriculum to the child rather than forcing the child to fit the curriculum, knowledge of materials and teaching approaches must be broad, and the teacher must be able to use that knowledge in relation to diagnostic abilities as well. While using developmental abilities, the teacher must be able to provide for learning of basic academic skills. In other words, standards must be maintained, and much more responsibility for this rests on the teacher than in schools where textbooks and other uniformly prescribed materials comprise the curriculum.

Probably few teachers exist who have all the desired characteristics, although professional growth in such a setting will bring many teachers progressively toward the required mixture of qualities. Therefore, especially during the early months of operation, the abilities of the various staff can be called on to complement each other. It will also be desirable, even in well-established developmental schools, to use this team-resources approach whenever helpful.

It would be advantageous if every teacher in charge of a class could have a paraprofessional aide and/or a parent helper. More activities could go on simultaneously with a helper, because, with the mixture of ages, any teacher assigned to the school must be able to maintain several activities at the same time. Specialists in music, art, and physical education would greatly facilitate the program and a librarian, or someone acting that role, is essential.

Physical Arrangement. Although a developmental school is not dependent on any specific arrangement of space, the program will be more compatible with some physical arrangements than with others. The self-contained classroom is the least well adapted physical arrangement although with some difficulty such a classroom could be used. More desirable would be a clustering of classrooms which could be opened into each other or which could be separated when desirable. Such an arrangement provides the possibility of cross-class activities but retains the stabilizing factor of an individual classroom.

Multi-purpose areas containing the library, media center, art center, music room, and gymnasium, would facilitate bringing together children with similar interests for selected activities. These areas also provide opportunities for children to exercise independence and responsibility.

A well-equipped outdoor playground is an extension of the classroom. No developmental primary school should be without one. The equipment should be challenging, but there should also be space for games and other activities which need no equipment. The outdoor playground does not need to be large enough for all children at one time. Ways can be found to regulate usage so that smaller groups are there at any one time.

A developmental school must have a workroom where teachers can produce materials to use with the children, such as games, puzzles, simple alphabet and number puzzles, and simple toys. This room needs permanent equipment, such as jigsaws and paper cutters, and supplies that do not have to be kept in every classroom. It requires a well stocked, supply cupboard.

Developmental Centers. Although knowledge does not fall into neat compartments, the classroom must provide some organized way for children to work and play together. This is done through setting up developmental centers where children can engage in reproductive play. Some developmental centers are planned to simulate real life experience. Some are relatively permanent and others will develop and change with the activities of the children. Some of the more permanent areas are the library-reading-research area, music area, listening-viewing-recording area, art and crafts area, dress up area, home-playhouse area, wood construction area, block building area, math area, and science area. (See Appendix C for materials which might be put in each area.) Any of these areas can be temporarily converted into a more specialized area. For example, the block area could become a space center, post office, supermarket, newspaper office, or any kind of vehicle, such as an airplane, boat or even a puppet theater. The dress up area could be turned into a stage, the listening-viewing area could become a television or radio station, and the science area could have animals part of the time, plants part of the time, or convert to a water play center part of the time.

Responsibility for changes in the centers would be shared. Sometimes the teacher would introduce new materials for a center. Sometimes, children's play takes a direction which could stimulate setting up a new center or transforming a center temporarily. The math center could temporarily become a time center with children learning about different clocks and what they can do in various lengths of time. The teacher, however, must see that there are new activities every day without waiting for changes to happen. The teacher actively sees that they do happen.

Evaluation. The developmental school would have a plan for continuous evaluation of the children's work. At the beginning of each year, developmental objectives would be determined for each child. A plan of record keeping would be developed, and evidence of behavior in relation to the objectives would be accumulated.

Role of Play in the Curriculum

Play has three major strengths in planning the curriculum for kindergarten and primary children: *(a)* its use of the child's curiosity about the physical environment, *(b)* its potential for dramatic and sociodramatic play, and *(c)* its potential for games with rules. If you accept these strengths and trust in the children's desire to learn, you can maximize their learning through play.

Curiosity About the Physical Environment. Capitalizing on the child's natural curiosity can aid in planning the curriculum during the years when children engage in productive and reproductive play. Direct experience with materials is indicated. An endless variety of materials can be placed in the developmental centers for children to explore. With kindergarten children, questions can be raised to extend ways they engage in exploration. After their explorations, discussion can enable the children to share their knowledge and observations. How much of the activity is verbal and how much is written depends upon the skills of the children. Gradually, with the youngest kindergarten children, the teacher would begin to write their observations down for them. Children could record them on tapes or in pictorial form. When children acquire reading and writing skills, they would copy what you have recorded or write their own records.

In its simplest form, the procedures we are discussing relate to objects, animals, materials and experiments. The children play with and use these things to find out what will happen or what they can do with them. However, the same motivation is used when five-year-old children prepare foods, or seven-year-old children prepare more complicated recipes and simple meals, when children make trips for specific information, and when consultants are invited into the classroom to share skills, materials or information. Children's curiosity should increase as they become more aware of how many interesting things there are in the world to discover. The use of curiosity for motivation is basic to a program that relies on play for learning. Curriculum content is controlled by the experiences available. Chapter Three provides assistance in developing experiences, especially during the productive play stage.

Curiosity is part of the child's motivation in the use of such materials as water, sand, clay, and paint, and in play with simple puzzles and construction toys. Teachers who want children to engage in these activities must make them seem attractive to the children and rely heavily on the children's own motivation to take care of the next step.

Dramatic and Sociodramatic Play. Dramatic and sociodramatic play provide the opportunity for children to interact with materials and with each other, to assimilate concepts, and to communicate on both verbal and nonverbal levels. Sociodramatic play, in particular, is an essential means by which children in the reproductive play stage learn how to relate their observations to both realistic and make-believe situations. Sociodramatic play also provides the best opportunity for the teacher to observe the kinds of feelings children have about themselves, how they relate to other children, what kinds of controls they have over their behavior, and how they have processed their experiences. Large blocks of uninterrupted time, ample materials, and freedom for children to pursue their own interests should be important parts of the developmental primary school.

An important aspect of sociodramatic play is that it integrates children's acquisition and processing of information, their acquisition of individuality, and their mastery of the social environment. Because individual children remain in control of their own behavior, they have the opportunity to practice being independent and responsible. Sociodramatic play is almost always related to children's physical and motor activities, since it involves creating props from blocks, art materials, and a variety of "junk."

From sociodramatic play, when children become a little older, come their more realistic creations, such as a ticket booth, the school supply store, or a fruit stand where real transactions take place in selling things to other children. Here academic skills can be practiced. After children's controls and cooperative abilities have improved, other activities develop, such as creative dramatics, puppet shows in which the puppets really assume roles and perform, and play-making in which the children actually perform.

Games with Rules. Games with rules would assume two very important roles in the developmental primary school: (1) in the group games and physical activities of the children, and (2) in classroom games involving academic and other skills.

The developmental primary school has an active program that uses developing physical abilities as well as social and cognitive abilities. Children would have opportunities to organize games and practice physical skills. Equipment should be available for learning skills, such as hitting a ball, skating, or playing basketball or jumping rope. All of these activities involve the whole body. Although the children will have learned some group games from neighborhood children, other group games should be taught at school.

Games will also assume an important teaching role in the classroom. In language arts, games can be created to teach word meaning, spelling, dictionary skills, and alphabet sequence. Mathematics games can be created to teach counting, addition and subtraction, comparing, classification, time, and measurement. In social studies, games could help in understanding social issues and feelings. These should be considered important learning activities, not just something to fill time, and should be planned into the schedule.

Toward a Developmental Primary School

The developmental primary school deliberately tries to provide the appropriate environment for children to allow them to be themselves and to develop at the pace and in the way that is best for them. It puts special stress on individual discovery, on first hand experiences, on play, and on opportunities for creative work. Knowledge in the developmental school is not neatly compartmentalized, and work and play are not easily distinguished from one another. It is a community in which children live first and foremost as children and not as future adults. Children whose needs are met as they progress through the different stages of their development and education have the best chance of becoming balanced and mature adults. They are also more likely to be able to contribute to and look critically at the society in which they are a part. Children who have these experiences are best equipped to cope with today's changing society and to cope with the future.

NOTES

1. Toffler, Alvin, *Future Shock,* (New York: Random House, 1970).

APPENDIX A

Child Competencies—Appalachia Preschool Curriculum

1. Forms concepts (example: concept of "same," "different")
2. Discriminates by sound
3. Discriminates by sight (example: 3-D and 2-D, shapes, colors)
4. Discriminates by touch
5. Sorts (groups and labels, categorizes)
6. Ordinates (by size, by number, by numerals)
7. Conserves (understands equality and inequality of sets through changes)
8. Measures (to estimate weight, distance)
9. Denotes spatial relationships
10. Judges physical and personal causation
11. Recognizes the passage of time
12. Recognizes familiar geographic and natural phenomena (e.g., lakes, clouds, thunder)
13. Uses imagination in play; pretends
14. Operates on quantity (adds subtracts)
15. Perceives from partial information
16. Remembers, recalls
17. Recognizes the social functions of language (i.e., that it permits people to relate)
18. Labels (attaches names to objects, feelings, events)
19. Explains (e.g., explains the function of something)
20. Describes (e.g., from a picture)
21. Articulates (can be understood)
22. Expresses feelings
23. Uses nonverbal cues (including facial, vocal, gestural)
24. Comprehends statements and questions
25. Uses typical sentence constructions
26. Uses language to seek new information (asks questions)
27. Furthers play by talking aloud
28. Recognizes others' expressed emotions

29. Constructs (i.e., with material requiring hand-eye coordination)
30. Copies
31. Draws
32. Uses body to express feelings
33. Controls large muscles (balance, coordination)
34. Controls small muscles (actions not covered in 29–31)
35. Initiates action (explores, is curious, starts things)
36. Plans actions (anticipates, assesses resources)
37. Persists in actions (despite distractions, completes)
38. Is self-reliant (e.g., dresses independently, washes, grooms, shows confidence)
39. Sustains health and safety standards (avoids dangers)
40. Accepts and tries new things (such as new foods and routines)
41. Waits a short time for something
42. Accepts some rules
43. Prefers particular activities (likes, dislikes)
44. Releases tensions (motorically and verbally)
45. Shows courtesy
46. Follows willingly the directions of a favored adult (such as a parent or teacher)
47. Responds to social as well as concrete reinforcement
48. Assumes appropriate social behaviors (shares, cooperates, makes positive social contacts)
49. Gets attention (to arouse interest or concern)
50. Maintains attention of others
51. Adopts the perspective of another (role plays, interacts with another's role)
52. Respects the individuality of others
53. Imitates the actions of a favored adult
54. Prefers the company of a "friend"
55. Feels secure with adults, although acts independently
56. Understands own place within the family
57. Understands who he/she is
58. Asserts own rights (especially against an instrusive "invader")

APPENDIX B

Suggestions for Field Trips and Excursions

1. Familiarize yourself with the trip area and the personnel to be visited.
2. Plan specific things to see. Plan with children so they know what they are looking for.
3. Be sure that young visitors will be welcome.
4. Arrange excursion in terms of time of day and week. Excursions taken the day before or after a holiday are frequently unsatisfactory.
5. Most excursions for preschool children should be neighborhood trips which do not require transportation.
6. Allow a generous ratio of adults to children so that children have ample time to observe what interests them.
7. Acquaint staff and helpers with the plans.
8. Before setting out on trip make sure that children take care of toilet needs and are properly dressed.
9. Know where toilets and drinking fountains are located if trip is outside neighborhood.
10. Plan opportunities for discussion of excursion in days to follow and provide appropriate props for dramatization.
11. Evaluate the excursion to know the strengths and weaknesses of your plan.

Suggested Trips
(Appropriateness will frequently be determined by distance)

airport	bus station
apiary	cabinet shop
bakery	cannery
barber shop	car wash
beach or waterfront	cereal factory
beauty shop	chicken hatchery
bird sanctuary	church organ, windows
boat piers	Christmas tree farm
building under construction	cider mill

city bus barn
city maintenance equipment
 at work
creamery
dentist's office
department store
depots
farm
farmers market
fire station
florist
garage
garden, vegetable or
 flower
garden store
gravel or sand pit
greenhouse
grocery store
hardware store
home maintenance and repair shops
 basement
 cement work
 paintings
 roof repair
 sodding

tree cutting and trimming
ice cream plant
irrigation dams and systems
kennel
letter box at corner
library
lumber yard
museum
newspaper office
orchards
park
pet store
pumping station
puppies, kittens and other
 small animals
restaurant kitchen
school points of interest
shoe repair shop
taxi dispatch office
teacher's house
train ride
t.v. and radio stations
woods, fields or streams
zoo

Resource People Who Might Visit Classroom

custodian
dentist
doctor
electrical maintenance men
fireman
forest ranger
hobbyist
 collectors
 puppeteers

librarian
musician
neighbors with pets
nurse
plumber
policeman
science instructor

APPENDIX C

Equipment

This equipment list has been developed so it can be used to select materials for use with nursery school, kindergarten and primary children. Each item is designated as 1, an essential item; 2, a desirable item; and 3, a luxury item. When items are not appropriate for an age they are designated NA.

Building and Construction Materials

	Nursery			Kindergarten			Early Elementary		
Suggested Items	1	2	3	1	2	3	1	2	3
Bin for lumber			x			x			x
Blocks									
Hollow (30)	x			x			x		
Parquetry, set		x		x			x		
Small table blocks, set									
(variety of types)	x			x			x		
Unit (150)	x			x			x		
Small flat boards to use									
with blocks		x			x		x		
Building sets									
Crystal climbers			x			x			x
Giant tinker toys			x			x			x
Lego	x				x		x		
Lincoln Logs		x			x		x		
Rig-a-jig			x			x			x
Rising Towers		x			x		x		
Tinker Toys		x		x			x		
Carpentry equipment									
Bench		x			x		x		
Clamps	x			x			x		
Drill and bits		x			x		x		

Suggested Items	Nursery 1	2	3	Kindergarten 1	2	3	Early Elementary 1	2	3
Hammers (2)	X			X			X		
Tape and ruler (3)		X		X			X		
Nails (assorted sizes)	X			X			X		
Nuts and bolts (assorted)	X			X			X		
Pliers		X			X			X	
Sandpaper	X			X			X		
Saws (2)	X			X			X		
Screwdrivers		X		X			X		
Screws		X		X			X		
Washers		X		X			X		
Cloth	X			X			X		
Corks (collected scraps)	X			X			X		
Foam rubber (collected scraps)	X			X			X		
Glue	X			X			X		
Lumber (assorted shapes, sizes)	X			X			X		
Paint, tempera (4 qts.)	X			X			X		
Shellac, clear (1 qt.)	X			X			X		
String		X			X			X	
Straws		X			X			X	
Tongue depressors		X			X			X	
Toothpicks		X			X			X	
Twine		X			X			X	
Wheels, wooden discs		X			X			X	
Yarn	X			X			X		
Dowels		X		X			X		
Alcohol, qt.			X	X			X		
Linseed oil			X	X			X		
Coping saw & blades (2)			X	X			X		
Smoothing plane			X	X			X		
Try squares (3)			X	X			X		
Monkey wrench			X	X			X		
Wall rack or cart for tools			X			X			X
Block attachments (steering wheels, etc.)		X			X				X
Toys to use with blocks (farm set, wooden airplanes, cars, boats; play people, wooden trucks)	X			X					X
Sturdy, rideable trucks that hold blocks	X			X					X

Dramatic Play

Suggested Items	Nursery			Kindergarten			Early Elementary		
	1	2	3	1	2	3	1	2	3
Animal costumes		x			x			x	
Small plastic figures	x				x			x	
Puppets (assorted)	x			x			x		
Stuffed animals	x				x			x	
Camping items									
Back pack			x			x			x
Blankets		x			x			x	
Camper truck			x			x			x
Flashlight		x			x			x	
Pup tent			x			x			x
Sleeping bag			x			x			x
Camp stove			x			x			x
Utensils		x			x			x	
Doctor/Nurse									
Bandages, band-aids	x			x				x	
Hospital gown & uniform	x			x					
Blood pressure gauge		x			x			x	
Stethoscope		x			x			x	
Mirrors		x			x			x	
Surgeon's mask		x			x			x	
Male and female grooming articles (combs, brushes, hand mirror, razor, soap, etc.)		x			x			x	
Aprons		x			x			x	
Bathinette			x			x			x
Bottle brush		x			x			x	
Broom, child size	x			x			x		
Dish cloth		x			x			x	
Dish pan		x			x			x	
Drainer		x			x			x	
Dry mop		x			x			x	
Dust pan		x			x			x	
Iron, wood	x			x				x	
Ironing board		x			x			x	
Pail	x			x				x	
Towels (bath, dish, etc.)	x			x				x	
Vacuum cleaner			x			x			x
Cooking and eating equipment									
Baby bottles (2)	x			x				x	

Suggested Items	Nursery			Kindergarten			Early Elementary		
	1	2	3	1	2	3	1	2	3
Cutlery (4 sets)	X			X				X	
Dishes (4 sets)	X			X				X	
Food container	X			X				X	
Food, pretend	X			X				X	
Utensils	X			X				X	
Dolls (boy and girl, multi-ethnic)	X			X			X		
Doll bed (28" x 14" x 10")		X			X			X	
Buggy and stroller			X			X			X
Baby clothes	X			X				X	
Doll house		X			X			X	
Dolls for house		X			X			X	
Doll house furniture		X			X			X	
Dress up clothing	X			X			X		
Furniture for Playhouse Area									
Bed and mattress (for child to lie on)		X			X			X	
Linens		X			X			X	
High chair		X			X			X	
Rocking chair	X			X				X	
Straight chair	X			X				X	
Clothes rack		X			X			X	
Curtains		X			X			X	
Dresser		X			X			X	
Hat rack		X			X			X	
Mirror (full length)	X			X			X		
Radio			X			X			X
Refrigerator (12" x 20" x 36")	X			X				X	
Rug	X			X			X		
Sink (12" x 27" x 24")	X			X				X	
Sofa		X			X			X	
Stove (12" x 16" x 24")	X			X				X	
Table (to seat 4)	X			X				X	
Telephones (2)	X			X				X	
TV frame		X			X			X	
Toilet training chair		X			X			X	
Office and School Play Items									
Attaché case			X			X			X
Chalk board		X			X			X	
Eraser		X			X			X	

Suggested Items	Nursery			Kindergarten			Early Elementary		
	1	2	3	1	2	3	1	2	3
Paper pads		x			x			x	
Pencils & erasers		x			x			x	
Typewriter		x			x			x	
Lawn mower			x			x			x
Paint brushes		x			x			x	
Paint cans		x			x			x	
Push broom		x			x			x	
Rake		x			x			x	
Tool box & kit (pretend)		x			x			x	
Sewing materials		x			x			x	
Model sets (airport, gas station, fire station, etc.)			x			x			x
Snap train sets		x			x			x	
Traffic signs		x			x			x	
Vehicles, large, sturdy, rideable (used also for block play)	x				x			x	
Vehicles, small, plastic or metal		x			x			x	
Store and storekeeping supplies		x			x			x	
Cash register		x			x			x	
Play money		x			x				
Shopping bags		x			x			x	
Shopping cart			x			x			x
Laundry set									
Old fashioned tub and washboard			x			x			x
Washer and dryer			x			x			x
Wooden cupboard (22″ x 20″ x 40″)	x			x				x	
Milk carrier & bottles		x			x			x	
Clothes bar (30″ x 36″)		x			x			x	
Clothes line & pins	x			x				x	
Clock, wooden		x		x			x		
Scales		x			x			x	

Apparatus for Physical Activity

Suggested Items	Nursery			Kindergarten			Early Elementary		
	1	2	3	1	2	3	1	2	3
Balance beam		x			x			x	
Balls	x			x			x		
Barrels		x			x			x	
Bean bags	x			x			x		
Bicycle pump	x			x			x		
Boards									
Resilient, for jumping		x			x			x	
Plain 6' x 8'		x			x			x	
Cleated 4' x 6'		x			x			x	
Boxes, large, scrounged	x			x			x		
Bridges, metal sawhorse type		x			x			x	
Climbing structures									
Old tires, empty electric reels, etc.	x			x			x		
Crates, packing boxes		x			x			x	
Digging hole		x			x			x	
Dollies, hand		x			x			x	
Fences, 6' lengths		x			x			x	
Hoops		x			x			x	
Ladder, sturdy	x			x			x		
Climbing net		x			x			x	
Platform with railing, ladder, sliding pole, etc.			x			x			x
Playhouse frame			x			x			x
Pulleys			x			x			x
Rope		x			x			x	
Sawhorses		x			x			x	
Seesaw		x			x			x	
Shovels, small, but sturdy	x			x			x		
Slide	x			x			x		
Steering wheel		x			x			x	
Step platforms	x				x		NA		
Stick horses		x			x		NA		
Swing set			x			x			x
Tumbling mats		x			x			x	
Wheel toys									
Tricycles (4)	x			x			NA		

Suggested Items	Nursery 1 2 3	Kindergarten 1 2 3	Early Elementary 1 2 3
Tricycle trailers	x	x	NA
Wagons (2)	x	x	NA
Wheel barrow	x	x	NA
Sand box and sand toys (see creative arts)	x	x	x
Skipping ropes	NA	x	x
Bats	NA	NA	x
Punching bag	x	x	x
Rocking boat	x	x	NA

Creative Arts

Suggested Items	Nursery 1 2 3	Kindergarten 1 2 3	Early Elementary 1 2 3
Aprons (bought or homemade) (6)	x	x	x
Beads for stringing	x	x	NA
Brushes ½"-1" thickness	x	x	x
Cans for cutting dough	x	x	x
Chalk (white and assorted colors)	x	x	x
Clay (gray and red)	x	x	x
Clothes pins for hanging work	x	x	x
Collage materials (scrounged)	x	x	x
Containers for clay, collage materials, paint, etc.	x	x	x
Cookie cutters	x	x	NA
Crayons, jumbo, (assorted colors)	x	x	NA
Crayons, regular		x	x
Drying rack	x	x	x
Easels, double, adjustable (2)	x	x	x
Community easel	x	x	x
Garlic press for clay	x	x	x

Suggested Items	Nursery			Kindergarten			Early Elementary		
	1	2	3	1	2	3	1	2	3
Glue white	x			x			x		
Hole puncher		x			x			x	
Kiln			x			x			x
Knives for clay		x			x			x	
Laces for stringing		x			x			x	
Looms, homemade for simple weaving		x			x			x	
Marking pens	x			x			x		
Masking tape	x			x			x		
Paint									
Finger	x			x			x		
Liquid tempera		x			x			x	
Powdered tempera	x			x			x		
Water colors (6 boxes)		x			x			x	
Paper									
Construction	x			x			x		
Kitchen shelf		x			x			x	
Cardboard	x			x			x		
Brown wrapping	x			x			x		
Crepe	x			x			x		
Frieze		x			x			x	
Manila	x			x			x		
Poster	x			x			x		
Tag board	x			x			x		
News print	x			x			x		
Paper bags	x			x			x		
Paper clips	x			x			x		
Paper cutter	x			x			x		
Paste (semi-liquid)	x			x			x		
Pencils (thick)	x			x			x		
Pie tins	x			x			x		
Plasticine		x			x			x	
Play dough (homemade)	x			x			NA		
Potter's wheel			x			x			x
Printing materials for play dough	x				x		NA		
Rolling pins (2)	x				x		NA		
Scissors:									
Rounded (left & right handed) (8)	x			x			x		
Semi-pointed (left & right handed) (8)	x			x			x		

Suggested Items	Nursery			Kindergarten			Early Elementary		
	1	2	3	1	2	3	1	2	3
Scotch tape	x			x			x		
Soap (for painting)									
Flakes	x			x			NA		
Liquid	x			x			NA		
Sponges (for painting)	x			x			NA		
Squeeze bottles		x			x			x	
String, twine, yarn	x			x			x		
Tongue depressors	x			x			x		
Tooth picks	x			x			x		
Wood pieces	x			x			x		
Chalk board	x			x			x		
Cloth: burlap, other	x			x			x		
Food coloring	x			x			x		
Flour	x			x			x		
Pins and needles	x			x			x		
Stapler	x			x			x		
Thumbtacks	x			x			x		
Sandbox (indoor and outdoor)	x			x			x		
Sand	x			x			x		
Sand/later play materials									
Brushes, large		x			x			x	
Containers (wide variety)	x			x			x		
Dishes	x			x			x		
Dishpans	x			x			x		
Floating toys and objects	x			x			x		
Funnels	x			x			x		
Hose		x			x			x	
Measuring sets	x			x			x		
Various									
Molds	x			x				x	
Pails	x			x				x	
Pitchers	x			x			x		
Scoops	x			x			x		
Sieves	x			x			x		
Later table		x			x		x		
Contact paper	x			x			x		
Dry mount press		x			x			x	
Rubber cement	x			x			x		

Suggested Items	Nursery			Kindergarten			Early Elementary		
	1	2	3	1	2	3	1	2	3
Laundry starch for papier-mâché		NA		x			x		
Wheat powder for papier-mâché		NA		x			x		
Charcoal	x			x			x		
Erasers: art gum	x			x			x		
Paraffin		NA			x			x	

Music

Suggested Items	Nursery			Kindergarten			Early Elementary		
	1	2	3	1	2	3	1	2	3
Auto harp		x			x			x	
Dancing clothes		x			x			x	
Records	x			x			x		
Record player	x			x			x		
Rhythm instruments									
Bells, cow, wrist, ankle	x			x			x		
Castanets		x			x			x	
Cymbals	x			x			x		
Drums, variety	x			x			x		
Maracas		x			x			x	
Recorder			x			x		x	
Sticks	x			x			x		
Tone blocks	x			x			x		
Triangles		x		x			x		
Tuning fork		x			x			x	
Wood blocks	x			x			x		
Other, homemade	x			x			x		
Piano			x			x			x
Chinese tom-tom		x			x			x	
Tambourine	x			x			x		
Tape recorder			x		x			x	
Xylophone		x			x			x	
Blank sheet music		NA			NA			x	
Chimes		x			x			x	
Clappers		x			x			x	

Suggested Items	Nursery 1 2 3	Kindergarten 1 2 3	Early Elementary 1 2 3
Finger cymbals	x	x	x
Gong	x	x	x
Marimba	x	x	x
Rattles	x	x	x
Sand blocks	x	x	x
Listening post (4–6 earphones and jacks)	x	x	x
Music books	NA	x	x
Abacus	x	x	x

Mathematics

Suggested Items	Nursery 1 2 3	Kindergarten 1 2 3	Early Elementary 1 2 3
Attribute blocks	x	x	x
Counters of various kinds	x	x	x
Cuisinaire rods	x	x	x
Fraction manipulatives	x	x	x
Food to cut	x	x	x
Measuring equipment, English and Metric			
Dry, units	x	x	x
Liquid, units	x	x	x
Tape	x	x	x
Rulers	x	x	x
Thermometers	x	x	x
Money, play	x	x	x
Nesting toys	x	NA	NA
Number games	x	x	x
Numerals, tactile	x	x	x
Shapes, sets of various materials	x	x	x
Objects, to examine likenesses and differences	x	x	x
Sorting containers	x	x	x
Timers			
Calendars	x	x	x

Suggested Items	Nursery 1	2	3	Kindergarten 1	2	3	Early Elementary 1	2	3
Clocks	x			x			x		
Egg timer	x			x			x		
Food timer	x			x			x		
Watch	x			x			x		
Weights (English and Metric)									
Standard pan balance		x			x			x	
Graduated cylinder balance			x			x			x
Bathroom scale	x			x			x		
Kitchen scale	x			x			x		
Spring scale			x			x			x
Plywood clocks, with manually operating hands	x			x			x		
Counting cubes		x			x			x	
Counting rods		x			x			x	
Games:									
Bead & number cards	x			x			x		
Card matching	x			x			x		
Numeral to numeral	x			x			x		
Number to numeral	x			x			x		
Dominoes	x			x			x		
Lotto matching sets	x			x			x		
Number bars	x			x			x		
Number trays	x			x			x		
Scoring games	x			x			x		
Pegboards	x			x			x		
Geo, set	NA			NA				x	
Cash register		x			x			x	
Flash cards		x			x			x	
Magnetic numerals and board		x			x			x	
Bingo		x			x			x	
Link numbers		x			x			x	
Skittles		x			x			x	
Other number games	x			x			x		

Science

Suggested Items	Nursery 1 2 3	Kindergarten 1 2 3	Early Elementary 1 2 3
Air experiments			
Balloons	x	x	x
Bellows	x	x	x
Bicycle pump	x	x	x
Bubble pipes	x	x	x
Kite	x	x	x
Squeeze bottles	x	x	x
Straws	x	x	x
Tubing	x	x	x
Animals (possible choices)	x	x	x
Birds			
Chickens			
Ducks			
Fish			
Gerbils			
Guinea pigs			
Hamsters			
Insects			
Silk worms			
Mice			
Rabbits			
Rats			
Snails			
Snakes			
Sponges			
Turtles			
Animal food	x	x	x
Eggs and incubator	x	x	x
Food and gardening			
Aprons	x	x	x
Children's cookbook	x	x	x
Various containers	x	x	x
Cotton	x	x	x
Dirt box or plot	x	x	x
Fertilizer	x	x	x
Food	x	x	x
Garden tools			
Child size hoe, rake,			
spade, etc.	x	x	x
Seeds	x	x	x

Suggested Items	Nursery			Kindergarten			Early Elementary		
	1	2	3	1	2	3	1	2	3
Plants	x			x			x		
Stakes and string		x			x			x	
Terrarium		x			x			x	
Watering cans		x			x			x	
Binoculars			x			x			x
Camera			x			x			x
Electricity									
Batteries, bulbs, wire, etc.	x			x			x		
Flashlights		x			x			x	
Magnifying glasses, hand	x			x			x		
Magnifying glasses, stand		x			x			NA		
Microscope		x			x			x	
Mirrors		x			x			x	
Prisms		x			x			x	
Liquids	x			x			x		
Dry ice		x			x			x	
Kettle		x			x			x	
Medicine dropper		x			x			x	
Sponges	x			x			x		
Inclined planes		x			x			x	
Magnets and nails, etc. to pick up	x			x			x		
Rubber bands	x			x			x		
Siphon		x			x			x	
Take-apart equipment (old typewriter, etc.)		x			x			x	
Minerals: rocks and stones	x			x			x		
Ant farm			x			x			x
Aquarium		x			x			x	
Bee hive			x			x		x	
Animal cages	x			x			x		
Cocoons		x			x			x	
Various cooking equipment	x			x			x		
Kaleidoscope		x			x			x	
Thermometers	x			x			x		
Watering cans		x			x			x	
Water table		x			x			x	
Compass	x			x			x		
Hot plate		x			x			x	
Iron filings		x			x			x	
Test tubes and beakers		NA			NA			x	

Suggested Items	Nursery 1 2 3	Kindergarten 1 2 3	Early Elementary 1 2 3
Tuning fork	x	x	x
Weather vane	x	x	x
Egg timer	x	x	x
Egg beaters	x	x	x
Globe	x	x	x
Pulleys	x	x	x

Perceptual-Motor

Suggested Items	Nursery 1 2 3	Kindergarten 1 2 3	Early Elementary 1 2 3
Puzzles	x	x	x
Building sets			
Crystal Climbers	x	x	x
Giant Tinker Toys	x	x	x
Lincoln Logs	x	x	x
Rig-a-jig	x	x	x
Rising Towers	x	x	x
Tinker Toys	x	x	x
Wooden beads	x	x	x
Matching games			
(Lotto, etc.)	x	x	x
Flannel board	x	x	x
Flannel board figures	x	x	x
Geometric solids	x	x	x
Magnetic board	x	x	x
Magnetized figures	x	x	x
Mechanical board			
nuts, bolts, locks	x	x	NA
Nests of rings or boxes	x	x	NA
Olfactory materials			
spices, foods, etc.	x	x	x
Parquetry blocks	x	x	x
Peg boards	x	x	x
Pegs	x	x	x
Sound cylinders	x	x	x
Tactile materials	x	x	x
Taste materials	x	x	x

Suggested Items	Nursery 1	2	3	Kindergarten 1	2	3	Early Elementary 1	2	3
Lego		X			X			X	
Picture dominoes		X			X			X	
Snap-and-play blocks		X			X			X	

Language Arts

Suggested Items	Nursery 1	2	3	Kindergarten 1	2	3	Early Elementary 1	2	3
Alphabet letters, tactile	X			X			X		
Books									
Permanent collection of 30	X			X			X		
Borrowed from library	X			X			X		
Easy to read	X			X			X		
Picture	X			X			X		
Poetry	X			X			X		
Resource books	X			X			X		
Camera		X			X			X	
Cassette tape player			X			X	X		
Chalkboard	X			X			X		
Felt board and pieces	X			X			X		
Films		X			X			X	
Filmstrips		X			X			X	
Games, simple, such as lotto, other picture games	X			X			X		
Language master		X			X			X	
Notebooks for dictated stories	X			X			X		
Pictures and posters	X			X			X		
Puzzles	X			X			X		
Records	X			X			X		
Slides		X			X			X	
Talking book unit		X			X			X	
Typewriter		X			X			X	
Writing materials	X			X			X		
Games: completion, story sequence, picture and lotto	X			X			X		

Suggested Items	Nursery 1 2 3	Kindergarten 1 2 3	Early Elementary 1 2 3
Frames, sorting by initial or rhyming sounds	x	x	x
Listening post	x	x	x
Puppets	x	x	x
Dramatic play materials	x	x	x
Wooden telephones	x	x	x
Viewmaster	x	x	x
Viewmaster reels	x	x	x
Textbooks	NA	NA	x
Reading charts	NA	NA	x
Wall strips	x	x	x
Wall cards	x	x	x

BIBLIOGRAPHY

Almy, Millie, ed., *Early Childhood Play: Selected Readings Related to Cognition and Motivation* (New York: Simon and Schuster, 1968).

Arnaud, Sara H., "Some Functions of Play In the Educative Process," *Childhood Education,* **51** (November/December, 1974), pp. 72–78.

Bettelheim, Bruno, "Play and Education," *School Review,* **81** (November, 1972), pp. 1–13.

Butler, Annie L., Gotts, Edward Earl, and Quisenberry, Nancy L., *Early Childhood Programs: Developmental Objectives and Their Use* (Columbus, Ohio: Charles E. Merrill, 1975).

Caplan, Frank, and Caplan, Theresa, *The Power of Play* (Garden City, N.Y.: Anchor Press/Doubleday, 1973).

Cass, Joan, *The Significance of Children's Play* (London: B. T. Batsford, 1971).

Clarizio, H. F., and McCoy, G. F., *Behavior Disorders in Children,* 2nd ed. (New York: Thomas Y. Crowell, 1976).

Cohen, Monroe, ed., *Selecting Educational Equipment and Materials* (Washington, D.C.: Association for Childhood Education International, 1976).

Day, Barbara, *Open Learning in Early Childhood* (New York: MacMillan, 1975).

de Grazia, Sebastian, *Of Time, Work and Leisure* (New York: The Twentieth Century Fund, 1962).

Dewey, John, *How We Think* (Chicago: Henry Regnery Company, 1933).

Erikson, Erik H., "Play and Actuality," Maria W. Piers, ed., *Play and Development* (New York: W. W. Norton, 1972).

Erikson, Erik H., "A Healthy Personality for Every Child," Millie Almy, ed., *Early Childhood Play: Selected Readings Related to Cognition and Motivation* (New York: Simon and Schuster, 1968).

Erikson, Erik H., *Childhood and Society, 2nd Ed.* (New York: W. W. Norton, 1963).

Freud, Sigmund, *Beyond the Pleasure Principle,* Standard edition, **18** (London: Hogarth, 1955).

Froebel, Friedrich, *Chief Writings on Education* Trans. S. S. Fletcher and J. Welton (London: Arnold, 1912).

Furth, Hans G., and Wachs, Harry, *Thinking Goes to School: Piaget's Theory in Practice* (New York: Oxford University Press, 1975).

Gesell, Arnold and Thompson, Helen, *The Psychology of Early Growth* (New York: MacMillan, 1938).

Gesell, Arnold, *The Mental Growth of the Preschool Child* (New York: MacMillan, 1926).

Gordon, Ronnie, "Playgrounds Can Be 'Experience Equalizers,' " *American School and University,* **46, 10** (June, 1973), 37–38 & 40–41.

Gotts, Edward E., Lawhon, Del, and Spriggs, Alice M., *Final Report: Marketable Preschool Education, 1975-76* (Charleston, W. Va.: Appalachia Educational Laboratory, 1976).

Gotts, Edward E., *Form for Rating Attainment of Early Childhood Competencies and Behavioral Performances* (Charleston, W. Va.: Appalachia Educational Laboratory, 1975).

Gotts, Edward E., and Taylor, Karin Oddsen, *Children's Activities Study (Play Study)* (Charleston, W. Va.: Appalachia Educational Laboratory, 1975).

Groos, Karl, *The Play of Man* (New York: Appleton, 1901).

Hall, G. Stanley, *Youth: Its Education, Regimen and Hygiene* (London and New York: Appleton, 1921).

Hall, G. Stanley. *Aspects of Childlife and Education* (London and Boston: Ginn, 1907).

Ilg, Frances L., and Ames, Louise Bates, *Child Behavior* (New York: Dell, 1955).

Kaplan, Max. "New Concepts of Leisure Today," *Journal of Health-Physical Education-Recreation,* **43** (March, 1972) pp. 43–46.

Lorenz, Konrad, "The Enmity Between Generations and Its Probable Ethological Causes," Maria W. Piers, ed., *Play and Development* (New York: W. W. Norton, 1972).

Lowenfeld, Margaret, *Play in Childhood* (New York: John Wiley & Sons, 1967).

Markun, Patricia M., ed., *Play: Children's Business* (Washington, D.C.: Association for Childhood Education International, 1974).

McFarland, Suzanne L. D., *The Effects of Play and Toy Stereotypic Value on Association Fluency of Kindergarten Children,* Unpublished Ed.D. Dissertation, Indiana University, 1976.

McLellan, Joyce, *The Question of Play* (London: Pergamon Press, 1970).

Montessori, Maria, *The Montessori Method* (New York: Bentley, 1964).

National Association for the Education of Young Children, *Play: The Child Strives Toward Self-Realization* (Washington, D.C.: N.A.E.Y.C., 1971).

Neuman, Eva A., "Observing and Planning for Play," ERIC No. ED **105 986,** 1974.

Omwake, Eveline B., "The Child's Estate," Millie Almy, ed., *Early Childhood Play: Selected Readings Related to Cognition and Motivation* (New York: Simon and Schuster, 1968).

Orthner, Dennis K. "Leisure Styles and Family Styles: The Need For Integration," *Journal of Health-Physical Education-Recreation.* **45,** (November/December, 1974) pp. 43–45.

Passantino, Erika D., "Adventure Playgrounds for Learning and Socialization," *Phi Delta Kappan,* **56,** No. 5 (January, 1975) pp. 329–333.

Pavenstedt, Eleanor, *et al., The Drifters: Children of Disorganized Lower Class Families* (Boston: Little, Brown, 1967).

Peller, Lili E., "Models of Children's Play," R. E. Herron and Brian Sutton-Smith, eds., *Child's Play* (New York: John Wiley, 1971).

Piaget, Jean and Inhelder, Barbel, *The Psychology of the Child* (New York: Basic Books, 1969).

Piaget, Jean, *Play, Dreams and Imitation in Childhood* (New York: W. W. Norton, 1962).

Rheingold, Harriet L., "Sharing at an Early Age," ERIC No. 093 **448,** 1973.

Robison, Helen F., "The Decline of Play in Urban Kindergartens," *Young Children* **26** (August, 1971) pp. 333–341.

Silberman, Charles E., ed., *The Open Classroom Reader* (New York: Random House, 1973).

Singer, Jerome L., *et al., The Child's World of Make-Believe* (New York: Academic Press, 1973).

Smilansky, Sara, *The Effects of Sociodramatic Play on Disadvantaged Preschool Children* (New York: John Wiley, 1968).

Sponseller, Doris, ed., *Play As A Learning Medium* (Washington, D.C.: National Association for the Education of Young Children, 1974).

Sunderlin, Sylvia, ed., *Bits and Pieces* (Washington, D.C.: Association for Childhood Education International, 1967).

Sutton-Smith, Brian, "Play as Variability Training And, As the Useless Made Useful," ERIC No. ED 084 **008,** 1972.

Sutton-Smith, Brian, "A Syntax for Play and Games," R. E. Herron and Brian Sutton-Smith, eds., *Child's Play* (New York: John Wiley, 1971).

Stern, W., *Psychology of Early Childhood* (New York: Henry Holt, 1924).

Stone, Gregory P., "American Sports: Play and Display," Eric Larrabee and Rolf Meyersohn, eds., *Mass Leisure* (Glencoe, Ill.: The Free Press, 1958).

Thomas, Alexander, *et al., Temperament and Behavior Disorders in Children* (New York: New York University Press, 1968).

White, Burton L., *The First Three Years of Life* (Englewood Cliffs, N.J.: Prentice-Hall, 1975).

Winnicott, D. W., *Playing and Reality* (London: Tavistock Publications, 1971).

RESOURCES

Ideas for Play Activities

Alkema, Chester J., *Puppet-Making* (New York: Sterling, 1972).

Association for Childhood Education International *Bits and Pieces: Imaginative Uses for Children's Learning,* (Washington, D.C., ACEI, 1967).

Association for Childhood Education International, *Cooking and Eating with Children* (Washington, D.C.: ACEI, 1974).

Austin Association for the Education of Young Children, *The Idea Box* (Washington, D.C.: National Association for the Education of Young Children, 1973).

Bordan, Sylvia Diane, *Plays As Teaching Tools in the Elementary School* (West Nyack, New York: Parker, 1970).

Caney, Steven, *Play Book* (New York: Workman, 1975).

Caney, Steven, *Toy Book* (New York: Workman, Inc., 1972).

Carlson, Ruth K., *Enrichment Ideas, Second Edition* (Dubuque, Iowa: William C. Brown, 1976).

Collier, Mary Jo, Forte, Imogene and MacKensie, *Kid's Stuff: Kindergarten and Nursery School Language Arts, Sciences, Social Studies, Math, Art, Music* (Nashville, Tennessee: Incentive, 1969).

Cook, Myra, Caldwell, Joseph, and Christensen, Linda, *The Come Alive Classroom: Practical Projects for Elementary Teachers* (West Nyack, New York: Parker, 1967).

Croft, Doreen J. and Robert D. Hess, *An Activities Handbook for Teachers of Young Children* (Boston: Houghton Mifflin, 1975).

Day, Barbara, *Open Learning in Early Education* (New York: Macmillan, 1975).

Dean, Joan, *Room to Learn: Working space, language areas and a place to paint* (New York: Citation Press, 1974).

Flemming, Bonnie Mack, et al., *Resources for Creative Teaching in Early Childhood Education* (New York: Harcourt, Brace, Jovanovich, 1977).

Forte, Imogene, et al., *Cornering Creative Writing* (Nashville, Tennessee: Incentive Publications, 1974).

Furth, Hans G. and Wachs, Harry, *Thinking Goes to School* (New York: Oxford University Press, 1975).

Gillies, Emily, *Creative Dramatics for All Children* (Washington, D.C.: Association for Childhood Education International, 1973).

Glass, Fredrica and Gross, Lela, *Calendar Capers* (Milwaukee: Bruce, 1965).

Horton, Lowell and Horton, Phyllis, *The Learning Center: Heart of the School* (Minneapolis: Denison, 1973).

McGavack, John, Jr. and LaSalle, Donald P., *Guppies, Bubbles and Vibrating Objects: A Creative Approach to the Teaching of Science to Very Young Children* (New York: John Day, 1969).

Machado, Jeanne M., *Early Childhood Experiences in Language Arts* (Albany, New York: Delmar, 1975).

Mayesky, Mary, Neuman, Donald, Wlodkowski, Raymond J., *Creative Activities for Young Children* (New York: Delmar Publishers, 1975).

Palmer, Bruce, *Making Children's Furniture and Play Structures* (New York: Workman, 1974).

Pitcher, Evelyn Goodenough, et al., *Helping Young Children Learn* (Columbus, Ohio: Charles E. Merrill, 1974).

Pugmire, M. C. Weller, *Experiences in Music for Young Children* (Albany, New York: Delmar, 1977).

Taylor, Barbara, *A Child Goes Forth* (Provo, Utah: Brigham Young University Press, 1970).

Vermeer, Jackie and Lariviere, Marian, *The Little Kid's Craft Book* (New York: Taplinger Publishing Company, 1973).

Wiseman, Ann. *Making Things—The Handbook of Creative Discovery* (Boston Toronto, New York: Taplinger, 1967).

Wylie, Joanne, *A Creative Guide for Preschool Teachers* (Racine, Wisconsin: Western, 1965).

Yawkey, Thomas Daniels and Eugene L. Aronin, *Activities for Career Development in Early Childhood Curriculum* (Columbus, Ohio: Charles E. Merrill, 1976).

INDEX